Advance Praise for Millennials' Guide to Management and Leadership

"Without a doubt, this book contains the most important messages for Millennials in the workforce. There may be other books that call for new ways of thinking for Millennial leaders, but until Jennifer Wisdom put her knowledge to paper, no other book has provided such a wise, research-backed guide complete with practical action steps. As a Millennial entrepreneur myself, I cannot recommend this powerful work highly enough, as it directly addresses the challenges that are unique to this group. For those that are struggling in the workplace, Dr. Wisdom lays out an approachable path for transformational change and her words are full of clarity and insight. For any emerging leader or manager, this book should be the first point of reference for all personal and professional interactions."

— Danielle Cuomo, MBA

"In her highly anticipated follow-up to *Millennials' Guide to Work: What No One Ever Told You About How to Achieve Success and Respect,* Dr. Wisdom nails it! With a keen awareness of the critical issues facing Millennials in the workplace and beyond, she doesn't miss a beat in this phenomenal guide. As Millennials quickly gain critical mass in the workforce and management, a book such as this is a welcome breath of fresh air. Given that Millennials have unique needs as a generation that vary drastically from those of the generations that preceded them, Dr. Wisdom provides a no-nonsense guide that is written with compassion, drive, and a deep desire to help Millennials thrive no matter what the challenge!"

— **Goali Saedi Bocci**, PhD, licensed clinical psychologist and author of *The Millennial Mental Health Toolbox* (PESI Publishing & Media, 2020).

"In her newest book, Dr. Wisdom offers guidance and support for Millennials currently, or attempting to obtain, managerial and leadership positions. In *Millennials' Guide to Management and Leadership*, Dr. Wisdom shares with readers a plethora of concrete tools—from visualizing and securing the managerial/leader job of their dreams to successfully developing a positive work culture. Readers can use this book to address specific issues as they arise or to gather a baseline understanding of effective elements of managing and leading teams. This resource will be of value to the inexperienced and seasoned manager/leader alike."

> – **Jennifer K. Felner**, PhD, MPH, San Diego State University (SDSU)

MILLENNIALS'
GUIDE TO
MANAGEMENT
&LEADERSHIP

What No One Ever Told you About
How to Excel as a Leader

WINDING PATHWAY BOOKS

JENNIFER P. WISDOM

Published by: Winding Pathway Books

WINDING PATHWAY BOOKS

ISBN (print): 978-1-7330977-3-4
ISBN (e-book): 978-1-7330977-4-1

Editing by: Margaret McConnell
Book Design by: Deana Riddle at Bookstarter, and Brian Sisco at 115 Studios
Photo Credit: Diego G. Diaz
For more information or bulk orders, visit: www.leadwithwisdom.com

Printed in the United States of America

Table of Contents

PART III. STAFF DEVELOPMENT

PART IV. STAFF CHALLENGES

PART V. COLLEAGUE CHALLENGES

PART VI. MANAGING UP

Introduction

In these uncertain times, it's more important than ever to apply our unique skills to make a positive difference in the world. We all have many strengths—our kindness, analytical skills, organization skills, or empathy—and many of us have considered serving as managers or leaders to help achieve goals, mentor others, and get stuff done. Add to this the challenge of being a Millennial, and being told all Millennials are lazy, entitled, or self-centered . . . and thinking about our career options can be confusing and frustrating!

I provided basic information about how to be successful at work in *Millennials' Guide to Work: What No One Ever Told You About How to Achieve Success and Respect*. If you've considered being a manager or leader, or if you are wondering if this is the right next step for you, *Millennials' Guide to Management and Leadership: What No One Ever Told you About How to Excel as a Leader* is the book for you. In my 20+ years of managing and leading as a Generation X, mentoring many young people in school and business, and working as a therapist for many others, I have a unique and practical perspective on helping you too become the best manager and leader you can be.

Let's start with the generational issues: Millennials were born between approximately 1980 and 1996. You followed Generation X (born 1965–1980), who followed the Baby Boomers (born 1946–1964), who followed the Silent Generation, also called Traditionals (born 1922–1945). Some people have said Millennials are confident, tolerant, and have a high sense of social awareness; others call Millennials entitled and self-centered. Millennials are also the first "digital native" generation, which is new for us Gen Xers and older who started on a Commodore 64 or a typewriter.

I'm always asked why I write for Millennials, and my answer is the same—you are the young people of today. You're the optimistic, adventurous—perhaps skeptical and unsure—people who will take over the country and the world. As practical as I am, I'm also aware Millennials are ALREADY half of the workforce as I write this in 2020. And by 2025, Millennials will be 75% of the workforce! Older generations can complain all they want, but a little secret: every older generation has complained about its young people. Let all the anti-Millennial stuff go. You do you, and if you want to be a manager or leader, I'm here to help you be the best manager and leader you can!

A few thoughts about managing and leading. Academics have had lots of discussion about the differences and similarities between management and leadership. Generally, *leadership* is the act of creating vision, inspiring people to follow and contribute, and providing inspiration to achieve the vision. *Management* focuses on the operations of the organization, including recruiting, training, and supporting people in their work; improving processes; and balancing time, cost, and scope of projects to achieve the overall vision. In reality, these distinctions are not particularly useful, especially in practice. Some people are better at one or the other, such as ideas people who aren't very practical or managers who get stuff done but aren't really ideas people. In general, people who lead should also be good managers, and good managers need to be good leaders. In this book, I'll use the words interchangeably and trust you to know what is most important for you.

The book is divided into sections to help you work through the main components of becoming a manager. For each area, there are 10 to 15 items to review or action steps you can take. You don't have to take them all at once; review the How to use this book section for suggestions about how to work with the action steps.

If you're familiar with *Millennials' Guide to Work*, you'll find a few of those sections are repeated here, but with a managerial twist. Some aspects of work—such as obtaining a mentor or coach, office romance, social media, feeling overwhelmed, and clarifying your values—are timeless and I've included them here as well.

Part I: Preparing for Management and Leadership gives you some background about becoming a manager/leader, including what they do, what skills are needed, identifying your style, and how to get help from a mentor or career coach. It also includes my absolute favorite, most important skill: *Challenge 12: Learn how to have difficult conversations.* If you only work on one skill from this book, this should be it.

We then move into challenges with ourselves in *Part II: Self-Management Challenges*. We've all had the feeling we are our own worst enemy . . . this section helps you deal with those parts of yourself you want to shape up, including starting a new manager/leader job, managing your time, and running a good meeting.

Part III: Staff Development helps you approach hiring, supervising, mentoring, and retaining staff as you get started. This is one of the most challenging new skills most managers and leaders have to learn—that balance in supporting your staff while also ensuring the work gets done.

Part IV: Staff Challenges addresses what to do when things go wrong—if your staff are late, don't take initiative, are disrespectful, or have low morale. As a manager/leader, you can generally turn these situations around.

What is work without colleagues? Developing strong relationships is important (See *Challenge 18: Build allies and friendships at work*), and sometimes there are challenges as well. *Part V: Colleague Challenges* addresses how to deal with colleagues who are gossipy, competitive, or who don't contribute.

Part VI: Managing Up discusses how to deal with your boss, your boss's boss, and everyone else more senior to you in your organization. This includes how to get mentoring or sponsorship from your boss, understanding hierarchy at work and when to go around it, and what to do if you are bullied, undermined, or want to ask for a raise.

Part VII: Strategy and Advanced Politics provides some information on how to manage organizational change, deal with seemingly impossible decisions, and figure out integrated work and life (hint: it's always a work in progress!).

Finally, *Part VIII: Career Challenges* addresses what to do when your career is stalled, if you're afraid, if you are considering moving on. It also provides strategies for dealing with success and learning from failure.

My experiences as a manager and leader have been educational, inspiring, frustrating, and overall, extremely fulfilling. I've learned so much, grown so much, and (I think) been able to help other people learn and grow to reach their potential. We're all works in progress, and I am hopeful this book will help you learn, grow, and reach your potential.

Please join my Millennials Facebook Page, or connect with me on social media.

Instagram: @leadwithwisdom
LinkedIn: linkedin.com/jenniferpwisdom
Facebook: facebook.com/leadwithwisdom
Twitter: @jenniferpwisdom
Website: www.leadwithwisdom.com

Jennifer P. Wisdom
March 2020

How to use this book

If you've read *Millennials' Guide to Work: What No One Ever Told You About How to Achieve Success and Respect*, you know how this works. *Millennials' Guides* are not books best read cover to cover. I encourage you to review the table of contents and identify a challenge you are currently having or recently experienced. Turn to those pages to start finding a solution!

Each challenge includes a brief description and at least 10 possible solutions that you may want to try. Many times, you can see success after trying one option. You'll see some solutions repeated across different challenges because they're likely to be helpful for many problems. For complex challenges, you may want to attempt several interventions at the same time.

It's important to have patience and give the solutions a little bit of time to work. Some ideas that you try won't solve the problem but will make it a little better—that's still success! If you don't feel comfortable trying a solution or if it works partially or not at all, try something else. Some of the solutions are very low risk, such as changing your expectations of the other person. Others can appear more challenging, such as directly discussing a concern with a colleague or asking for a raise from your boss. Start with solutions that feel like lower risk to you and work your way up to more challenging solutions.

The few basic rules of work will never steer you wrong—especially as managers and leaders:

1. Never say anything bad about anyone at work to anyone at work. (Do your venting at home or with friends.)

2. Write emails and chat messages as if they will be printed in the newspaper, broadcast on social media, or used in a court case (because they might be).

3. Be honest *and* diplomatic with everyone, including yourself.

4. Be patient. Sometimes people are working on your behalf to make things better and you don't even know it.

5. Be curious about yourself and seek constant self-improvement.

6. Remember that we all have struggles. Be kind and respectful.

As you work through possible solutions, you'll get better at reading situations, responding to people you work with, building networks, and applying solutions effectively. There will sometimes be political situations in which there is a game being played around you that you don't fully get. Observe, be patient, clarify your own boundaries, and learn. The more you know what you want, the more you'll be able to achieve your goals. If you're not sure what you want, that's okay too— that's a perfect place to be while you're in your 20s and 30s. The goal of the strategies in this book is to help you develop skills that will serve you well as you continue to move forward at work.

Each of you reading this book is a unique person with talents to share with the world. My hope is that this book can make it easier for you to do so. Good luck improving your work life!

Part I.
Preparing for Management and Leadership

Challenge 1.
What managers and leaders do

The terms leadership and management are often used interchangeably although they are distinct concepts with distinct characteristics. In most roles, you will need to demonstrate both management and leadership skills. Here's some basic information about leadership and management.

1. **Leadership** is the act of creating vision, inspiring people to follow and contribute, and providing inspiration to achieve the vision. Management focuses on the operations of the organization, including recruiting, training, and supporting people in their work; improving processes; and balancing time, cost, and scope of projects to achieve the overall vision. For example, a leader sets the organization's path and provides the vision for how the different functions across the enterprise can interact and integrate to achieve the desired future. A manager makes sure the project has resources, equipment, staffing, and permits for the quality goals to be achieved.

2. **Leadership can be viewed as the "influencing" part of management; management can be the "organizing" and "completing" (or process) parts of leadership.** Not all leaders are good managers, and not all managers are good leaders, but both roles can benefit from skills in the other's area. Managers are the people in charge of employees and the facilities they work for. As a manager, your job is to plan and promote the daily schedule of employees and the business; to interview, hire, and coordinate employees; create and maintain budgets; and coordinate with and report to senior managers in the company.

3. **Management guru Peter Drucker discusses five things managers do:** (1) Sets objectives and decides what work needs to be done; (2) Organizes work into manageable activities and determines who will do what; (3) Motivates staff to complete the work and communicates feedback and guidance to them; (4) Establishes targets to interpret performance; and (5) Develops employee skills and talents.

4. **Managers and leaders often make hard decisions and have difficult conversations.** They sometimes have to lay off or fire staff, let people know the goals weren't met, or provide performance feedback. It is possible to avoid hard decisions and difficult conversations, but that will set you and your team up for failure.

5. **Leaders and managers need to understand the link between vision and action.** They need to be able to see a vision and understand concrete steps to accomplish it. Leaders tend to focus more on vision but can be stymied if they don't have a realistic sense of what it takes to get the vision accomplished. If managers don't understand the vision, it's harder for them to direct and motivate workers to accomplish it.

6. **Both managers and leaders must be effective at prioritizing.** Whether prioritizing goals, tasks, or steps, it's important to be able to separate what's important from what is not.

7. **Leaders and managers need to be able to listen to others.** Whether it's understanding instructions from those higher up, collaborating with your peers and colleagues, or hearing concerns from your team, it's important to help people feel that they have been heard and to be able to respond appropriately to what they're telling you.

8. **Leaders and managers should be willing to take responsibility for their team's performance** and to manage internal problems within the team while respecting their team members' autonomy.

9. **Leaders and managers should prioritize their company's mission and their staff's success**—while also remembering their own career trajectory, professional development, and advancement.

10. **Leaders and managers should be able to clearly communicate their vision and disseminate information and instructions.** It's also important for them to know when the messages aren't getting heard (and instructions aren't being followed), so they can adjust strategies.

See also: Challenge 2: Why be a manager or leader

Challenge 3: Skills needed to be a good manager and leader

Challenge 83: Making sense of your career

Take action: What are the skills and talents you bring to the table that are consistent with being a manager or leader? Which of these activities listed here do you anticipate will be challenging for you?

Challenge 2.
Why be a manager or leader?

Leaders and managers are the backbones of business. In short, they dream big dreams and get things done. If that's not exciting enough, here are more reasons to consider becoming a leader or manager.

1. **Leaders and managers help their teams learn and grow.** If you like mentoring, helping others learn, and celebrating others' success (as well as your own), this could be a great choice.

2. **You want more responsibility? You got it!** Being in charge of a team—whether manager, leader, or both—gives you responsibility not only for your work, but for the work of your team. You can choose to hold them to a high standard and enjoy their progress.

3. **Millennials often want to make a difference in the world.** Good news: Managers and leaders can have greater influence and impact because of their roles. This responsibility means you're able to make more change, solve more problems, and achieve more.

4. **Leaders and managers have much more visibility**—both good and bad—than non-managers and non-leaders. For me, one of the things I missed the most when I became a leader was anonymity. I didn't realize how much I had been content to be unseen—or how satisfying it was to represent my team and my department!

5. **Increased salary.** Most fields pay managers and leaders more than those who aren't managers and leaders. That's good for your student loans (or your bottom line!).

6. **Managers and leaders often have opportunities for training** that are not available to others. Training could be in technical skills (like finance or programming) or on managerial/leadership skills, such as goal setting, negotiation, communication, equity, and strategy. Keep learning!

7. **Most of us think we communicate well.** Being a manager/leader puts that assumption to the test. Working with teams to share goals, identify and assign tasks, and manage challenges are a great way to hone your communication skills.

8. **If you are achievement-oriented,** management and leadership is often a great way to get things done and see progress from your work. For achievement-focused people, these positions provide more opportunity to achieve your goals.

9. **Leaders and managers can make their vision become real.** Those who lead innovative companies and departments, entrepreneurs, and others can collaborate to ensure a vision becomes a reality. Leaders and managers also get to celebrate success in a way that feels especially satisfying. Success means so much more when you have helped a group of people achieve more than they would have and possibly more than they thought they could.

10. **Leaders and managers can leave a powerful legacy.** Even in the most challenging positions, you can demonstrate what it's like to be a good leader, teach others, and share in success.

See also: Challenge 1: What managers and leaders do

Challenge 3: Skills needed to be a good manager and leader

Challenge 73: Career uncertainty

> **Take action: What attracts you to being a manager or leader? What about your past managers made you think they were good at their job? What would make you hesitant to become a manager or leader?**

Challenge 3.
Skills needed to be a good manager and leader

There are numerous skills important for being a good manager and leader. Here's a brief list.

1. **Know yourself.** It's a lifelong process to learn your strengths and weaknesses—and to be able to work with people who complement your strengths and push you to become better. The key is to find work at the intersection of what you like doing and what you're good at. Get better at knowing yourself by observing what you do well and less well, noting what you enjoy and don't enjoy doing, and by asking others for their perspectives. See resources on getting to know yourself in the For further reading section.

2. **Motivate yourself and others.** How do you motivate yourself? If you can't motivate yourself, it's hard to motivate others. Cultivate motivation in yourself to keep reaching your goals and practice motivating others.

3. **Solve problems.** Problems aren't what gets in the way of work—problems many times ARE the work. Seeing problems as puzzles or opportunities and being able to persevere to get really good at problem-solving will serve you well. Practice!

4. **Think big.** Wherever you are, you'll likely encounter someone saying, "That's the way we've always done it." You can choose, however, to think big and find new, better, more efficient or more effective ways to do things. Learn from the people who came before you and then you can really make stuff happen.

5. **Learn from failure**. We all experience setbacks or failures. It's important to use these lessons as learning opportunities. We can identify what went wrong and what we learned. Then get back up and keep going!

6. **Build networks**. Managers and leaders don't work solo, so they need to build networks and know when to ask for help. Thankfully having a good network with lots of give-and-take makes it easier to ask for help. Networking with others at your level, more junior to you, and more senior than you can all be a great way to make getting things done easier.

7. **Mentor others**. Work today requires a fascinating confluence of technical skills (e.g., finance, programming) and other skills, including getting along with others, communicating clearly, and learning from feedback. For many managers and leaders, mentoring and training others so they can learn as much as possible is a treasured part of the job.

8. **Public speaking**. Managers and leaders are much more likely to give presentations and to need to speak up in front of others. In fact, your likelihood of needing to speak in public increases as you rise through the ranks. If you're uncomfortable with public speaking, like many people are, you can start small by checking out Public Speaking Project online, Toastmasters online, or practicing at home.

9. **Address biases**. We all have biases and assumptions based on how, where, and when we grew up and all of our experiences since. Being a good manager and leader requires that you're always reassessing your biases (including implicit biases, which suggest that we can act on the basis of prejudice or stereotypes without intending to) and assumptions so you're not embarrassing yourself. It's a big world out there and being able to balance learning from experience while not overgeneralizing from those experiences is a key skill.

10. **Learn politics.** Sometimes people don't want to deal with politics at work—they don't like being "political" or view "playing politics" as negative. Once you're a manager or leader, however, you can't stick your head in the sand and pretend politics don't exist. At a minimum, you should be aware of what's going on around you politically to ensure you protect your team and take care of your career. Whether you choose to observe or intervene and "play politics" is up to you. Learn about politics by observing others, asking your mentors and trusted colleagues, and reading up on the topic. See recommendations in the For further reading section.

11. **Be adaptive.** We've probably all heard that the only thing constant is change, and most places of work are constantly changing, whether with staff coming and going, new technology, new contexts, or new priorities. Remaining flexible is key!

12. **Stand up for your team.** A key role for any manager or leader is to ensure your team has what they need to get their work done well. This includes making sure you as the boss stand up for yourself and your team, keep them from being bullied, and ensure they have the resources, motivation, and training needed to do the work.

13. **Demonstrate the value of diversity, equity, and inclusion.** Everyone starts a job with unique strengths, experiences, and skills. Championing and valuing diversity, equity, and inclusion isn't only the right thing to do—it makes your team stronger and more effective.

14. **Practice discernment.** This means choosing carefully, thoughtfully, and conscientiously; gathering information before making judgments; and sharing information judiciously.

15. **Listen to others, find your voice, and help them find their own voices too.** You'll need to learn from others—that's how

the best people get better. At the same time, it's important to find your *own* voice. And to use it.

See also: Challenge 1: What managers and leaders do

               Challenge 7: Developing/determining your managing/ leadership style

               Challenge 10: When and how to obtain a career coach

Take action: Which of these skills are you strong in? Which could use some work? Identify one or two skills and how you will improve your strength.

Challenge 4.
How to prepare to become a manager or leader

What can you do if you're thinking about becoming a manager or leader, but you're not sure you're ready to apply for a new job or take the plunge? Lots! Read on . . .

1. **Lead from where you are.** Regardless of your position, you can start to act like a leader, which means keeping the team focused on goals, helping find solutions, facilitating conflict, and staying positive.

2. **Work as part of a team.** Use your time now to get better at working with others. Even if your colleagues have different backgrounds, perspectives, motivations, or ideas, the goal is to find something you have in common and find a way to be successful together. Becoming a manager or leader doesn't mean you no longer have to work as a team; it makes teamwork even more important.

3. **Read widely.** Whether you read articles, how-to books, biographies, personal accounts of leadership, or scientific articles about management, all of these are enormously valuable. Consider targeting your reading for specific skills, like negotiation, strategy, or building teams. Practice skills that you learn.

4. **Reflect on what you're reading.** Consider what applies to your current situation, what you might do in situations discussed, and what the authors are stating that might be helpful to you. Practice skills that you learn.

5. **Build your network** with individuals at your level, more senior to you, and more junior to you. Network widely through all areas of your field. For example, if you work in finance, get to know not only other finance people, but also people in sales, marketing, product development, human resources, administration, and leadership.

6. **Join professional associations** related to your field and read their newsletters or magazines. This will help you get a different perspective of the field and understand current issues. Attend conferences or online programs if possible and remember to build your network.

7. **Volunteer for projects or tasks** that entail more responsibility or opportunities to learn more about the organization or field. For example, sitting on some committees provides a chance to learn about other areas of the organization outside your own, and to possibly increase your network.

8. **Review your resume or CV** to identify what it shows about your preparation for management or leadership and ask someone else to review it as well. Rather than describing only *what* you did, ensure you indicate your *impact* or the amount of funds or people you worked with. For example, instead of "Planned quarterly reports meeting," you could say, "Supervised staff of three and $20k budget for quarterly reports meeting for 50 attendees."

9. **Identify whether additional education would be helpful.** There are options of bachelors, master's, or doctoral degrees in your field, a Master's of Business Administration for general business acumen, or certificate programs in specialized subjects. There are also plenty of opportunities to learn for free—including from top universities—through online programs such as EdX and Coursera.

10. **Improve your communication skills.** Periodically ask for feedback on your writing—yes, including emails!—to identify

how to be more impactful. Whether your work calls for analytical writing, persuasive writing, descriptive writing, or critical writing, work to get even better.

11. **Be aware you will often need to make decisions without all of the information.** Practice reflection after decisions to determine what you did well and not as well, what information could have been helpful, and what you learned for next time.

12. **Understand the needs of your customers** (or clients or patients) and how to improve business processes. Identify ways to improve processes and improve customer experience. Anyone who can make clients happier, streamline processes, and hopefully save money in the process is definitely an up-and-comer.

13. **Demonstrate loyalty to your organization.** This doesn't mean you have to swear to be there forever or overlook any malfeasance, but it does mean you are working for the good of the organization. If you have concerns about how something is unfolding, speak about its impact on the organization. Taking the bigger picture and demonstrating you care about the organization's success is important.

See also: Challenge 1: What managers and leaders do

Challenge 3: Skills needed to be a good manager and leader

Challenge 5: How to break into management and leadership

Take action: What steps can you take now to move forward?

Challenge 5.
How to break into management and leadership

At some point, many of us feel like we can do more, we can take on more responsibility, and that we'd like to lead. Work on preparing for management roles (see Challenge 4), and then see which of the following make sense for you to keep moving on up!

1. **Ask.** Clarify your interest and aspirations, create a brief statement of why you want to become a manager (see *Challenge 2: Why be a manager or leader?*), and ask about being considered for a leadership or management role. You can talk with your boss, speak to a mentor, confer with a colleague, or chat with someone in Human Resources about your interests. Ask them for feedback and recommendations on how to be more competitive for management positions.

2. **Identify your company's leaders.** Use the organization chart or ask around to find out who senior staff are. Then look them up on social media, read their bios, and follow or link to them. Notice how they progressed through their career and note any items of interest that could be conversation starters, such as where they grew up or their alma mater.

3. **Be prepared to have a conversation when you run into a senior person in your company.** Introduce yourself briefly (name, position, tenure at the company, boss's name), thank them for the opportunity to work there, and say something positive—perhaps about something in their background that you found interesting or comment positively on something happening within the company. If the meeting is a hit, you may want to suggest getting together for a quick coffee conversation. Make sure to let your boss know.

4. **If your company has a management training program, apply for it.** If there are any internal management roles you are interested in, apply for them.

5. **Join professional organizations** in your field or affiliate with federal organizations and volunteer to take on leadership roles. Your visibility and success in those organizations can be very helpful to clarifying your management and leadership abilities in your company.

6. **Talk with your mentor(s) or trusted colleagues about your interests** in becoming a manager or leader and ask them for their perspective on how you could increase your profile and visibility.

7. **Conduct informational interviews** with people in roles you find interesting. Ask for 20 minutes of their time and prepare questions such as, How did you get into this role? What do you like about leading? What advice do you have? Be sure to thank them, in writing if possible.

8. **Volunteer for assignments or projects** outside of your normal duties, especially those that are cross-department (rather than within-department). These will provide you with a more comprehensive view of the organization and opportunities for networking and finding mentors. It also increases (hopefully!) the number and breadth of individuals who can put in a good word for you.

9. **Consider additional training**—and sharing with your boss that you are pursuing this additional education. There are options of bachelor's, master's, or doctoral degrees in your field, a Master's of Business Administration for general business acumen, and certificate programs in specialized subjects. There are also plenty of opportunities to learn for free—including from top universities—through online programs such as EdX and Coursera.

10. **Attend organizational networking or social events** to learn about the organization and others in it. Ask individuals what they do with the company and what they like, and generally get to know them.

11. **Consider bringing on and training an intern or volunteer.** Show off your management skills!

12. **With tact, volunteer to help your boss solve some of their problems.** You could say, "I want to make sure I'm doing the right thing here. Is there anything on your plate I could help with?" You will definitely learn more about what managers and leaders deal with. You also may build a better relationship with your boss.

13. **Know when it's time to move on.** If you've exhausted your opportunities at your current organization, it might make sense to consider transferring to another organization.

See also: **Challenge 1: What managers and leaders do**

Challenge 3: Skills needed to be a good manager and leader

Challenge 4: How to prepare to become a manager or leader

Take action: How would you frame your current experience in a cover letter or resume to support your managerial aspirations? Write it down and start working on it today!

Challenge 6.
Want more responsibility

It's hard to get a management job without management experience, and it's hard to get management experience without a management job. Same as it ever was. But not impossible to crack! You can demonstrate you are ready for a management/leadership position by taking on more responsibility. Here's how.

1. **Organizations sometimes send mixed messages about responsibility:** As a junior employee, you are expected to work hard under someone else's supervision. In order to be promoted, you must also somehow demonstrate initiative, independent thought, and responsibility. Recognize these mixed messages and identify opportunities to move between them.

2. **Volunteer for projects or tasks that entail more responsibility or opportunities to learn more about the organization or field.** For example, sitting on some committees provides a chance to learn about other areas of the organization outside your own, and to possibly increase your network.

3. **Talk with your boss about your interest in managing/leading,** and ask for projects where you could take on more responsibility. Be prepared to describe what your strengths are or what you would like to learn. Ask your boss questions about the opportunities, such as what they anticipate you'll learn and who you could get to know better.

4. **Join professional associations related to your field** and read their newsletters or magazines. This will help you get a different perspective of the field and understand current issues. Attend conferences or online programs if possible and remember to build your network.

5. **Look for stressed coworkers and offer to help them out.** Make sure you don't take on too much of other people's responsibilities, but helping someone out in the short term is a nice way to learn something new and build your network.

6. **Talk to someone you trust outside of work** for ideas on how to demonstrate responsibility at work.

7. **Study up on an area of interest for you.** An acquaintance of mine who works at a financial services firm started reading about blockchain, and through casual conversations about her interest, her boss asked her to teach the team about it. If it's related to work and you enjoy it, learn more about it!

8. **Talk to your colleagues about what kinds of responsibilities they have.** See if there are opportunities to do similar tasks in your current job.

9. **Be proactive.** Sometimes you don't have to wait for permission—if you see something that needs to be done, do it! Make sure you're not stepping on others' toes or reaching out too far, but most workplaces appreciate a little extra organizing and picking up tasks that are falling through the cracks. (Note: Never volunteer to clean the refrigerator in the break room or you will be expected to do it forever.)

10. **Do your research:** Identify areas of need in your department or organization's mission, and look into where the organization can get better at client outreach, retention, sales, or marketing.

11. **Keep at it!** Even if your first idea doesn't get approved, don't lose hope. Fortune favors the bold.

See also: **Challenge 9: When and how to obtain a mentor**

Challenge 13: Set professional goals

Challenge 25: Commit to continuous self-improvement

Take action: What do you want to be responsible for? What would it look like? Start dreaming, then start doing!

Challenge 7.
Developing/determining your managing/leadership style

There are plenty of opportunities to learn more about your management and leadership style, ranging from more structured or academic opportunities to more casual or introspective choices. Common leadership models can be useful for thinking of how one wants to lead. Note that you can exhibit characteristics of more than one model.

1. **Notice what brings you joy and what stresses you out.** What are you good at? What elements of your job are you good at, even if you don't like them? What needs do you have? What do you like and not like about your own supervisors? Thinking through these questions can help you identify what your own style might be.

2. **Consider taking a course to help you understand different management styles and what makes sense for you.** Plenty of formal courses about management are available, including through business schools and psychology programs.

3. **It's important to find your own leadership style,** even though the popular image of leadership is of the charismatic, inspirational leader. There are many kinds of leaders.

4. **Be aware that your leadership approaches will change over time** depending on your growth, the organization, current opportunities, and other factors. Every situation will help you gain experience to inform the approach you take for your next leadership challenge. The longer you are in leadership, the more comfortable you become maintaining a set of core

personal values and strategies that can guide your different leadership approaches.

5. **Authoritarian leaders** are those who provide clear instructions (commands) to others and have strong expectations for what the staff should be doing. Authoritarian leaders typically make decisions without input from the group, which can helpful in emergency situations or where the leader is more knowledgeable than the staff. In a more negative scenario, however, this type of leader can be viewed as controlling, less creative in decision-making, and as creating hostile environments or staff rebellion.

6. **Democratic leaders** offer guidance to staff, and also ask staff to participate in decision-making. Typically, staff with democratic leaders feel like they're a part of the team, contribute high-quality work, and demonstrate high commitment to the group. There may be somewhat less productivity, as group decision-making requires time, but overall staff tend to be happier.

7. **Laissez-faire leaders** are those who offer little or no guidance to staff and let them make their own decisions. This can be helpful with a team of expert staff, but it often leads to poorly defined roles, low motivation, and low productivity.

8. **Situational leaders** understand that each situation is different and requires a different approach. They provide the tools to lead using a situation-by-situation approach that assesses the nature of the task and the nature of the relationship with the worker.

9. **Strengths-based leaders** consider the strengths of each individual on the team or in the work unit. Leaders identify staff strengths and assign work by engaging people on projects that align with their strengths and that allow staff to effectively complement each other's skills.

10. **Transformational leaders** integrate their qualities and abilities to demonstrate authenticity, build and sustain morale, create culture change, model behavior for others, establish a collaborative mindset within the group, and empower workers to make decisions without micromanagement.

11. **Servant leaders** are those whose priority is to serve and enrich the lives of others and to create a more just world. Common traits of servant leaders include listening, empathy, stewardship, foresight, persuasion, conceptualization, awareness, healing, commitment to the growth and development of people, and building community.

See also: **Challenge 1: What managers and leaders do**

Challenge 15: Starting a new job as a manager or leader

Challenge 83: Making sense of your career

Take action: What styles here are consistent with your approach and values? What are aspects of these styles you would like to demonstrate more?

Challenge 8.
How to interview for a manager or leadership job

Once you are being considered for a job, you'll likely need to have a phone, online, or in-person interview. Although many people stress about the interview because you are being judged for your fit for the job, an interview is also your opportunity to check out the company and to see if you are interested in working for them. Preparation and practice will go a long way toward being seen as a top candidate!

1. **Prepare for your interview by reviewing the company, its products or services,** its leadership team, and if possible, the team you're applying to work with. If you know anyone who works at the company, ask questions about what it's like to work there. You may want to find out the company's approach to social responsibility, environmental sustainability, diversity and inclusion, and upward mobility.

2. **Regardless of your personal style, dress similarly to others who work at the company** in the level of seniority you're interested in. If you're not sure, dress more conservatively. You can always loosen up or show your tattoos once you have the job .

3. **If you can get information in advance on whom you will meet,** check out their social media or their profile on the company webpage so you will have information about their role in the company and any background information that may be useful (such as if you went to the same college). You don't have to mention anything about your homework in the interview, but it might come in handy, and it will definitely help you feel more confident.

4. **A few basics you likely already know:** Show up early. Show up alone. An executive I know told me about an interview candidate she was considering hiring, only to find that the candidate's parents were waiting in the lobby. And of course, be nice to everyone.

5. **Prepare for questions you will likely be asked and practice how you will answer them.** Common interview questions for mangers include: (a) Tell me about your experience managing others. (b) Why do you want this manager/leader position? (c) Tell me about a time when you had a management challenge? (d) How do you tend to communicate with your supervisor? (e) How do you manage stress? (f) What do you see as challenges for you in this position? Consider also such perennials as (g) What attracts you to this company? and (h) Where do you see yourself in five years?

6. **Prepare for a few "situational" questions that you are likely to be asked,** such as (a) tell me about a situation when you had an ethical dilemma, (b) tell me about a time when you failed, or (c) tell me about a time when you addressed conflict with a peer or staff member.

7. **Make sure to always tie your answer to the questions back to the job you're interviewing for.** For example: "Working on the committee was extremely fast-paced, and I was able to regularly and consistently turn around deliverables on tight deadlines. I imagine this skill will be helpful in the Manager position during the peak seasons of work when quick decisions are necessary."

8. **Prepare questions to ask the interviewer.** For managerial and leadership positions, these can include: (a) Can you tell me about the challenges my predecessor faced in this position? (b) What can you tell me about the team I would be inheriting? What strengths and challenges do they have? (c) Can you give me some examples of the most and least desirable aspects of [the company's] culture? (d) How do you define and measure success for this position? (e) What do you think will most surprise me about this job? (f) Why do you love coming to work in the morning? (g) (at end

of interview) Now that we've discussed my qualifications, what concerns do you have about my fit for the position? (h) (at end of interview) What are the next steps in the hiring process? Or When can I expect to hear back? Or What is the anticipated hiring date?

9. **In the interview, focus on the work.** Interviews are generally not a good time to ask about salary, vacation time, or other benefits unless the interviewer brings them up. In some companies, however, salary is not a taboo to discuss in the first interview. This is a tough decision, but by the time people are talking about start dates and contracts, that's a good time to discuss salary.

10. **If the interviewer wants to move forward with an offer, they may ask you about your start date or salary expectations.** It would be good to have a general idea of what you are looking for, but you don't have to negotiate on the spot. A good response can be, "When do you need an answer?"

11. **Always be nice to everyone you meet on an interview.** When you complete the interview, write thank-you letters to everyone you meet. I prefer handwritten as they make a bigger impact, but you could email them. Make sure you don't write everyone the exact same letter; find a way to personalize each one.

12. **Practice interviewing** with someone you trust who has been employed in a similar kind of job. Ask them to comment on your handshake, your eye contact, your tone (speak up!), and the content of your answers.

13. **Even if you ace the interview, you may not get the job and you may not hear any feedback.** That doesn't mean you did anything wrong. You can follow up with an email or phone call to request the status of your application for the position or to request feedback, but don't take it personally if you don't hear back.

See also: **Challenge 4: How to prepare to become a manager or leader**

Challenge 11: Clarify your values

Challenge 15: Starting a new job as a manager or leader

Take action: Think back to your last job interview (or discussion about a job if you haven't had an interview). What would you have done differently knowing what you know now? How can you use that information to improve the next time around?

Challenge 9.
When and how to obtain a mentor

Sometimes we all need help. The next few challenges identify the differences between a mentor and coach, and a therapist, including when you might need each of these, how to find one, and how to work with them. A mentor is someone who is committed to your growth and professional development. Typically, mentors help you learn what you need to know on the job and how to improve. A mentor is different from a coach in that a coach typically is paid and has very structured meetings focused on a specific goal.

1. **A good first step to finding a mentor is to figure out what you would like help with:** general professional advice, sticky situations, technical skills, advancement, and/or something else. Then you can start looking for someone who is especially knowledgeable about that area.

2. **See if your organization has a mentoring program,** new employee orientation, or early career networking meetings. Those are excellent places to find mentors. You might consider starting one if one doesn't already exist.

3. **Your mentor should act in your best interests with you.** Ideally, your mentor has your best interests and professional development in mind, but they are human too and may be interested in learning information from you or steering you in certain directions. If you feel your mentor is not acting in your best interests, you may want to step back and reassess.

4. **Respect your mentor's time.** Be on time and prepared for meetings. Do your homework first (don't ask them to tell you things a simple

Internet search would uncover). You may want to bring a written list of what you want to discuss.

5. **Follow up on your mentor's advice.** There are few things a mentor loves to hear more than "Your advice was so helpful. It really made a difference."

6. **Be aware that it's rare to find a single mentor who can meet all of your needs.** You may find one person who can help you with general professional advice, and another one who can advise on sticky situations. Go slowly on questions, and ask your mentor how they would like to proceed.

7. **Some mentorships last a lifetime, others for a short time.** If you need to end a mentoring relationship for whatever reason, it's always polite to thank the person for being there for you and let them know how much they have helped you.

8. **Help your mentor out when you can.** Send them news items or articles you came across that they might be interested in, or pass along non-confidential information they might find helpful to their goals. Ask them directly how you can help them.

9. **If you find a mentor isn't particularly helpful, be specific and ask for what you are looking for.** Mentors want to be helpful and will likely let you know if they can't help on a specific topic.

10. **Pass it on.** Regardless of your position and seniority, you know something someone doesn't. Be kind and mentor others. It will help you build positive, collegial relationships, and it will make the world a little friendlier for all of us.

See also: **Challenge 10: When and how to obtain a career coach**

Challenge 12: Learn how to have difficult conversations

Challenge 18: Build allies and friendships at work

Take action: Who mentors you? What's one step you can take right now to get the mentoring you would like?

Challenge 10.
When and how to obtain a career coach

Coaches are experts, usually paid, who help you tackle certain problems. Coaches are less likely to have any conflict of interest, as their primary goal is helping you achieve what you want to achieve. They are typically action-oriented and want to help you achieve change. This is different from a mentor, who often is a volunteer and who offers less structured support. A coach is also different from a therapist, whose primary focus is on coping and healing.

1. **You can find coaches through the American Psychological Association** (apa.org), the International Coaching Federation (icf. org), your state psychological association, and by searching online. Note there is no standard training or certification for coaches. Good to ask around and get a referral.

2. **Consider what you want in a coach.** You may want a coach who is certified as a coach or licensed as a psychologist, someone who is a professional in your field (e.g., finance, medicine), or all of the above. Look for a coach who has experience working with people at your level of seniority and with the kinds of problems you would like assistance with. If you're not sure, just ask.

3. **When you contact a prospective coach, ask about their style.** Some coaches have a warm, supportive style, whereas others have a more direct and confrontational style. If you have a preference, let them know and ask if they can accommodate.

4. **Ask about the prospective coach's strategies.** Do they have a formal assessment or interview before you begin? Do they tend to have a similar structure for each session? How do they consider homework? How do they balance inquiry and advice-giving?

5. **If cost is important, ask about how the coach charges for services.** Many coaches offer a "bundle," such as a single price for five or 10 sessions. Be sure to ask about what happens if you do not complete all sessions; you may be able to take a break but often will not be entitled to a refund. Find out in advance whether your workplace may support the cost of a coach.

6. **Be clear on what you want from a coach.** Usually coaches will help with dilemmas (such as whether to apply for a new job or not) or puzzles (such as how to build a better relationship with your boss or how to better balance work and life). If you're not sure what you want, then let the prospective coach know that and ask for assistance.

7. **Coaches ask a lot of questions, and they help you uncover answers in yourself.** Most coaches assume you are resourceful and talented in managing your own life. Don't be put off if the coach asks lots (and lots!) of questions, but if you prefer a more directive style, let them know.

8. **A coach should never discount the significance or importance of your challenge.** If you feel dismissed or talked down to, end the relationship and find someone who completely supports you.

9. **Many coaches assign homework.** Work with them on what you are comfortable with. Often the homework is for you to think through challenging issues or to practice strategies discussed in coaching sessions. You'll get more out of coaching if you do the homework.

10. **Coaches will provide you with feedback** regarding how you present within the session; for example, if you are brusque, late, or reject feedback, you will likely receive that feedback. If it is hard for you to receive feedback, let the coach know and ask to work on that.

11. **Be curious about yourself and be open to learning.** Coaching can be an effective way to help you reduce frustration and improve your skills!

See also: **Challenge 9: When and how to obtain a mentor**

Challenge 18: Build allies and friendships at work

Challenge 57: Obtaining mentoring/sponsorship from your boss

Take action: Do you know anyone who has worked with a coach? Ask around to see what their experiences are before you decide this is right for you.

Challenge 11.
Clarify your values

Some of us value a competitive environment that keeps us motivated, whereas others want a collegial and friendly environment. Some people don't mind specified work times, and others bristle at anything that feels like micromanagement. Often, we don't even consider our values until they are being challenged in some way. Values are statements of what we find important, valuable, or useful. Taking some time to clarify what we authentically value and where we draw the line can be important to guide us as we move forward in our careers.

1. **Often employers are looking for values** such as dependability, positive attitude, professionalism, loyalty, motivation, honesty, and adaptability. Starting with those values, how do you feel you measure up? How important are those values to you?

2. **Ask friends and family members who know you well** what they value and identify anything that feels true for you.

3. **Review values statements for your organization** and for other similar organizations to identify what feels right for you and what doesn't feel right for you.

4. **Consider difficult situations in your past** when you've had to make a decision. What principles guided your decision? What beliefs did you rely upon? If you can't recall a difficult situation or identify principles and beliefs you considered, it may point to a need to be more present or to begin documenting your experiences.

5. **Ask a trusted colleague about their values** and how they apply their values in day-to-day work.

6. **Consider whether your spiritual, religious, or cultural beliefs/ experiences** may impact your professional values.

7. **Consider what has prompted you to be concerned about values**: Is someone pressuring you to do something that goes against your values? Are you uncomfortable with an aspect of a work requirement or your work environment? Do you feel like you need to have clarity? Understanding *why* you want to clarify your values might give you some direction.

8. **A conversation about values is also a good time to consider your future**: Do you see yourself continuing in your field as a worker or as a manager? It's okay if you're not sure now. If you know you prefer one or the other, though, it's helpful to keep that in mind as you move forward because you will have decision points along the way where you need to choose a direction.

9. **When you are faced with a situation at work that is challenging, try to identify what is most important for you**: to do the right thing, to be fair, to help others, to be right, to avoid trouble? How might these preferences reflect your values?

10. **Know that your values will likely become clearer over time**, and trust that you are on the right path.

See also: **Challenge 13: Set professional goals**
            Challenge 22: Learn how to say no

> **Take action: What are your values? Where did you pick them up? Take notice of values that come from society, family, or religion and decide if you will keep them as your own or create new ones.**

Challenge 12.
Learn how to have difficult conversations

At various points in this book, I suggest you talk with your boss, a trusted colleague, or a mentor about a problem. This section provides some guidance on how to have these difficult conversations in a way that is respectful while keeping curiosity open to identify how to best proceed. Keep your values and goals in mind for difficult conversations. For more information, see the classic books *Difficult Conversations: How to Discuss What Matters Most* by Douglas Stone, Bruce Patton & Sheila Heen and *Crucial Conversations: Tools for Talking When Stakes Are High* by Al Switzler, Joseph Grenny, Kerry Patterson, and Ron McMillan (listed in the For further reading section).

1. **Don't avoid difficult conversations.** As author Tim Ferris said, "A person's success in life can usually be measured by the number of uncomfortable conversations he or she is willing to have."

2. **First identify what the issue is and what you would like the resolution of this conversation to be.** Maybe you're having a problem with a colleague, and you want to discuss it with a mentor. Find a way to describe the colleague problem succinctly, and ask for what you would like from the mentor. You could say, "I'd like to hear several ways to approach this situation" or "I'd like to hear what you would do if you were me."

3. **Recognize that in every conversation there is often a difference between what people think, what they say, and (if the conversation takes place in writing) what they write.** Starting with you, try to track the difference between what you say and what you're thinking. Keep in mind there are often comments you may think that should not be *said* or *written* at work.

4. **Consider that we all have different experiences because we focus on different things,** and we interpret the same events differently based on our past experiences and our values. For example, you and your boss may differ on what is meant by a "draft" report, and you may turn in something more "drafty" than your boss wanted.

5. **Approach each difficult conversation with a goal of each person getting some of what they wanted.** If you approach as all-or-nothing (you get everything you wanted and they get nothing), you are much less likely to have productive conversations (or to get what you want from them) in the future.

6. **Demonstrate that you are trying to understand what the other person is saying.** Pay attention, nod, or let them know how you are interpreting what they are saying. For example, you could say, "I want to make sure I understand. You are saying . . . ?" You could also elicit their perspective by asking something like, "I know you wanted to discuss our relationship. Why do you think it's tense?"

7. **Blame is not generally helpful** if you're looking for an answer or for a change. Blame also makes it look like you're not trying to resolve the situation, only trying to avoid responsibility. Try to stay away from blame and stick to the point.

8. **Whenever possible, use data to support your points.** Look up the information about how these situations are typically handled and the expected outcomes of how you propose to handle the situation.

9. **Be careful of taking action based on assumptions.** It's often best to go into a difficult conversation with a lot of questions about the other person's behavior or intentions. If you want to share with the person the impact of their behavior on you, you could say, "When [x] happened, I assumed [y]. Is that true?" or "When you [x], it was confusing to me. Could you help me understand what you meant?"

10. **You may want to practice difficult conversations with a friendly partner** beforehand. Anticipate what the other person might say

and practice how you might respond to various comments.

11. **Consider the extent to which you let your feelings be involved** in the conversation. Some people suggest all work conversations should be objective and emotionless; others (like me) believe that it's okay to let people know how you feel. ("I wanted to talk with you about yesterday's meeting. When you called me out, I felt embarrassed. Can we discuss how to do this differently next time?")It is important to not let your feelings take over.

12. **If you get upset or angry in a conversation, you can ask for a break** or suggest you continue the conversation at another time. That's a better choice than crying or yelling at someone. If you do cry or raise your voice, ask for a break and then go back to the conversation when you're more composed.

13. **Observe difficult conversations**—in person, in movies, eavesdropping on the subway—and identify what works well and what doesn't.

14. **Recognize that you will make mistakes**—we all do. Pick yourself up, identify what you learned, and keep going.

See also: **Challenge 9: When and how to obtain a mentor**

Challenge 22: Learn how to say no

Challenge 24: Manage and overcome overwhelm

Take action: What's a conversation you've been avoiding? What's one step you can take today to address the issue?

Challenge 13.
Set professional goals

Now that you're a manager or leader, you'll likely want to set goals for both your professional mission and for your own career development. Here's how.

1. **Identify the areas in which you would like to set goals**, such as for your professional mission as a manager/leader, career development goals that are likely separate from but overlapping with your current position, as well as other goals such as networking, fitness, financial, and others. You may also be able to double-dip; for example, goals to increase your professional network and to exercise could both be addressed by joining your organization's running group.

2. **Consider your Big Life Purpose**—why you believe you are on this planet—and then set big goals from there. Don't worry if they're too big; you'll grow into them!

3. **Set SMART goals**: Goals that are specific, measurable, achievable, realistic, and time-bound (they have a deadline).

4. **Set goals that have a variety of challenges**: some may be easy to reach, and others can be stretch goals, which require you to go beyond your comfort zone to work harder. Too many easy goals and you won't be challenged enough; too many stretch goals and you may get too discouraged.

5. **Set goals that have a variety of timelines**: some that can be achieved within weeks; others within a month or two; and big goals to be achieved within a year or two. Consider breaking big goals down into smaller chunks with shorter target dates for completion.

6. **Consider if there are impacts of setting official work-related goals** (e.g., for your organization, funded project). Ensure you collaborate with key people on goals that are not only about you.

7. **Ask people you admire about their goals** and ask about their goal-setting process.

8. **Sometimes goals may need to change.** Make sure you don't change goals every time you're discouraged or feel like you've reached a dead end—be thoughtful and consider what's best for you.

9. **Once you put your goals together, create plans to reach them.** Put them in your calendar or appointment book so you will remember.

10. **Be a leader you would like to follow.** If there's something you don't like about your organization, work tactfully to improve it. Listen to others, communicate clearly, stay positive, have empathy, and be constructive.

See also: **Challenge 9: When and how to obtain a mentor**

Challenge 14: Start seeing yourself as a manager/ leader

Challenge 18: Build allies and friendships at work

Take action: How will you take action toward your goals today? What is one thing you can do to clarify your goals and move toward them?

Challenge 14.
Start seeing yourself as a manager/leader

We've all heard about "fake it 'til you make it," but how does that apply to becoming a manager or leader when you're not sure how to behave or you might even feel like a fraud? Here are some suggestions for how to truly act like a manager and leader and to see yourself as a manager and leader—whether you have the title yet or not!

1. **Leaders and managers demonstrate confidence** because others on the team look to them for assurance that things are going well, that everything will be okay, and that they are safe. Demonstrate confidence that the goals are achievable, that the team can accomplish even more than they think they can, and that you believe in your team.

2. **No one likes someone who shirks responsibility.** Being a leader or manager doesn't mean it's okay to sit back with your feet up on the desk and just watch other people work. It's important to make sure you are doing your part to not only ensure the work is being done but to make sure the team has enough resources, that you're protecting them from any politics or interruptions, and that you're keeping your eyes open for opportunities to help them learn and grow.

3. **Dress the part.** This varies widely by company and industry, from extremely casual to very formal. It's important to see how those senior to you dress and to find a way to manage your appearance that is consistent with what the general expectations are *and* authentic to who you are. Although it's important to demonstrate your identity through your appearance, there are often ways to be authentically yourself while also demonstrating you are leadership material.

4. **It's important to demonstrate fairness,** even though we all have friends at work, and people we like or don't like. Sometimes all it takes is having a good discussion about the pros and cons with someone else to work through your ideas and ensure you're acting fairly.

5. **Communicate effectively.** Send concise and informative emails without sarcasm or snark. Write reports fully, showing your work and your analytical process. Whatever kind of writing your work requires, do it well.

6. **If you don't know about implicit bias, check it out.** Implicit bias suggests that we can act on the basis of prejudice or stereotypes without intending to and without realizing we have them in the first place. There are surveys available online to test our implicit bias. Whether you discuss them with a mentor or a therapist or through self-study, it's important as a manager and a leader that you hire the best person for the job and that you treat people fairly.

7. **Be the change you would like to see in your organization.** If you don't like something, choose to investigate how it came to be that way, and what the levers are that can change it. Use your power— even if it's limited—for good. Choose to set a positive example.

8. **Use who you are and your path to this position as an asset.** Many of us have felt embarrassed about our humble backgrounds, especially when surrounded by people with more impressive college or family connections. Others went to a prep school and Ivy League college. No matter how you got to this position, sharing your path and struggles with others can be an inspiration to them to continue to push themselves to excel.

9. **Find opportunities to build your resilience, negotiation skills, networking skills, patience, and communication skills.** Every moment can be a learning opportunity, even the most challenging moments (especially the most challenging moments!).

10. **Be consistent.** No one likes a hypocrite, and it's important to "walk the talk" (make your behavior consistent with what you suggest others do). It's helpful for others to know what to expect from you, whether it's that your words and actions are dependable, that you're not going to fly off the handle, or that you show up when you say you will.

11. **Be authentic and diplomatic.** Sometimes people think being "authentic" means they can say whatever occurs to them without regard to others' feelings or perspectives. I recommend instead a diplomatic authenticity, where you speak up and speak out, but do so in a way that is always professional and respectful.

12. **Take responsibility for yourself and the actions of your team.** This means you are clear about what you expect of yourself and of your team, and that you are actively creating conditions that facilitate you and your team in reaching goals. When your team is successful, give them credit. When you screw up, acknowledge it, and use the opportunity to learn.

See also: **Challenge 3: Skills needed to be a good manager and leader**

Challenge 11: Clarify your values

Challenge 83: Making sense of your career

> **Take action: What is one thing you can do today to reinforce your view of yourself as a manager/leader? Do it!**

Part II.
Self-management challenges

Challenge 15.
Starting a new job as a manager or leader

It's your first day as a new manager or leader! How exciting! You'll want to set the right tone and get to work. Here are some suggestions to do just that.

1. **Make a list of why you wanted the job and what your goals are.** File it away to look at in 3 or 6 months.

2. **Consider using humor to deflect tension,** such as by referring to yourself as "the newbie" and letting people know you're new when you ask questions. First impressions are important!

3. **Create a list of your questions for the first day and first week,** including finding the bathroom, cafeteria, payroll, etc. and bring them up as appropriate.

4. **Read the excellent resource *The First 90 Days: Critical Success Strategies for New Leaders at All Levels*** by Michael D. Watkins, which walks you through how to approach a first experience in a leadership role.

5. **You may want to consider obtaining a coach or discussing with your mentor** about starting a new job, including goal setting, network building, and achieving early wins.

6. **Introduce yourself kindly and generously to everyone you meet.** At this point, you don't know who they are, and you never know where they will be in the future.

7. **Be prepared to answer questions about where you were before you started this job.** If you took time off or had a difficult experience before starting this job, practice what you will say so that you can say it breezily until you get to know people better.

8. **Remember the individuals who interviewed you** and when you see them at work the first time, say something kind.

9. **Consider how you'll introduce yourself to your new staff.** Ideally you can introduce yourself casually the first few days, and then have a meeting of all of your staff together to conduct a more formal introduction, including letting them know who you are and your approach to the position. Give them an opportunity to ask you questions—it's a great opportunity to help them learn who you are.

10. **Consider also what you do not want to share at first,** whether it's your family/living situation, why you left your last job, or your level of ambition. People will be curious and want to learn who you are. Consider how you respond.

11. **Allow time for reflection.** It's easy to hit the ground running, but you want to make sure you're headed in the right direction! At least once a week, take some time to review what you've learned and ensure you're on the right track.

12. **Reward yourself with something pleasant** after you finish your first day, whether dinner with your partner or friends, a special dessert, or something else. You did it!

See also: **Challenge 7: Developing/determining your managing/leadership style**

Challenge 13: Set professional goals

Challenge 58: How your boss likes to receive information

> **Take action: When was the last time you started a job? What would you have done differently? Make note and identify how you'll put your best foot forward now!**

Challenge 16.
Understand your organization and its mission

As a leader or manager, you represent the organization. It's important to understand what the organization stands for, what it expects of its leaders, and what it expects of its employees so you can be effective.

1. **Review your organization's mission statement** and those from similar organizations to identify what makes your organization different from others.

2. **Read whatever you can about the organization**, including its internal-facing press (such as a company newsletter/email, memos on the company website), externally facing press (like public relations releases), annual reports, and history (search Wikipedia or Google news reports).

3. **Pay attention in meetings and conversations** to glean more information about the organization: How does it select leaders? How long do people typically stay with the organization? What does the organization value in its leaders? If you're not sure, ask.

4. **Observe the organization's culture**: Is it primarily focused on creativity, marketing, technology, financial success, or something else? Its focus could be a good fit or a poor fit for its products and services, and knowing this can help you identify how you can most contribute.

5. **Ask a trusted colleague about their perspective on what is important to the organization** and what aspects of organizational culture are consistent and inconsistent with your colleague's values.

6. **Pay attention to how you feel in the organization's spaces**. Are its workspaces welcoming? Are there areas for staff to gather

informally? What kinds of art or posters are on the walls? Do people seem relaxed, focused, stressed, angry? Understanding how the space feels to you can help you understand the organization's culture and its people.

7. **Take a look at the organizational chart and identify who is responsible for what.** Sometimes it's helpful to ask people about reporting chains and responsibilities and compare that to what is on the official organizational chart. Are middle-level managers strong and independent, or do they seem eager to always agree with the boss? This can give you clues regarding how you should act—coming in strong, or starting more slowly.

8. **Consider how people communicate.** Is communication formal or more casual? Do people talk seriously about issues in the organization? Do employees discuss financial issues and competitors or stay focused only on their narrower scope? Are colleagues respectful to each other? Are leaders respectful to their staff? Generally it's good to understand the current ways of communication so you can decide whether you want to fit in or stand out by communicating similarly or differently.

9. **Understand gatekeepers, whether formal or informal.** Assistants, administrators, or others are often tasked with managing low level situations or limiting access to a higher-up. Sometimes they have developed power beyond what might be expected, and it may seem that they are keeping you from connecting with senior people. Learn who gatekeepers are and develop positive relationships with them. If they see the value to their boss in what you are requesting, that will make your access easier.

10. **What does the organization consider problematic?** For example, some organizations are more formal, and its leaders indicate disapproval of goofing off or sloppiness. Others are overly perfectionistic and consequently may miss opportunities for innovation. If you identify which leaders are most influential in

the organization, that may help you understand what behaviors, attitudes, and strategies are supported and not supported.

11. **Take notes on these aspects of the organization and periodically review your observations and reassess.** Things will look different when you change positions, when someone new arrives, or when there is another disruptive action in the environment.

12. **Remind your staff of their part of the larger mission and purpose of your organization** to help motivate them and understand their relevance.

See also: **Challenge 1: What managers and leaders do**

Challenge 12: Learn how to have difficult conversations

Challenge 56: Understanding hierarchy at work and when to go around it

Take action: Identify one resource to learn more about your organization – the Internet, Wikipedia, a long-time employee, a colleague – and start asking questions.

Challenge 17.
Understand your team – including your boss and your staff

We all think bosses are mysterious people, until we become one. Similarly, getting to know our staff at work can help us—and them — be more successful. It's helpful, especially as we move into management and leadership positions, to understand our whole team.

1. **Learn as much as you can about your team without stalking them.** Check out their social media, their bio on the company page, press articles, podcasts, and anything else you can put your hands on easily. This will give you a better sense of who is on your team and where they're coming from. Learn about your team, including what they enjoy and dislike about their jobs, where they excel, how they communicate, and what drives them nuts.

2. **Help your team learn about your style and how it impacts others.** Are you a joker (whose jokes don't always land?) or a perfectionist (who can make others feel like they're never good enough) or very direct (which can come across as blunt or rude)? Whatever your style, encourage them to speak up if they have any questions or concerns. And when they do speak up, use it as an opportunity for both of you to learn and grow.

3. **Understand your team's story of who they are.** Teams often have a story about their history or their role in the organization, such as, "Since we bring in the most money for the organization, we are at the top of the heap" or "Our group's work is always underappreciated," or "Our glory days are behind us." Once you understand your team's story, identify the impact of that story on their work, and how you can improve it if it needs strengthening.

4. **As a manager, your responsibility to your staff includes providing clear guidance on what is expected,** helping staff get barriers out of the way, ensuring they have resources they need, and providing feedback so they can excel. Identify the ways this can work for your team.

5. **Understand how your team's performance is evaluated.** Review this process with your team so that they understand how their performance is evaluated. Take a look at the structure for performance reviews, and discuss with your team so expectations are very clear.

6. **Ask your staff how you can best help them** (without doing their job for them!). Ask your team to share their strengths with you and to make suggestions about how to improve work or how they can be more effective.

7. **Learn how your team perceives its primary goals.** That will help you understand how you can support them better, increase effectiveness, or facilitate change.

8. **Learn how your team is and isn't working together.** Even the most talented individuals can sink a team if they're not communicating, coordinating, and collaborating.

9. **Accept that a big part of your job—if not your *only* job—is to make your bosses look good.** Understand that this is your mission.

10. **Identify what would be most helpful to your boss.** You can always say to your boss, "I want to make sure I'm addressing the most important things for you," and then either share your list or ask them to share with you what's important to them.

11. **Keep personal and business relationships separate within your team.** Avoid any perception that you are playing favorites.

12. **One universal truth: No boss likes to be blindsided.** Make sure you keep your boss informed of problems and the solutions you've

begun so they can provide advice or at least start managing the situation with *their* bosses.

13. **If your boss is an "attack the messenger" kind of person,** after the tense moment has passed, ask them how they'd like to receive bad news and if there's anything you can do to make the process go easier. Let them know you of course want to minimize bad news, but you'd like to see how you can handle things better next time (even if they're the one who flew off the handle!).

14. **If your boss is a micromanager,** keep good notes and provide a list of all of your activities each time you meet with them. A table of activities and status can be extraordinarily useful in helping micromanagers understand that you're on top of all of your duties.

15. **Help your supervisors and supervisees help you help them.** Share your strengths with your supervisors and suggest ways you can be helpful to them. Nearly every supervisor loves ideas that improve financial performance, cut costs, or publicize successes. Help your supervisees be more effective by sharing with them your goals and what you need from them.

See also: **Challenge 14: Start seeing yourself as a manager/ leader**

Challenge 18: Build allies and friendships at work

Challenge 24: Manage and overcome overwhelm

Take action: Get to know your colleagues—professionally. Come up with a go-to question that always works, like "What have you been working on?" or "What are you looking forward to?" and start asking.

Challenge 18.
Build allies and friendships at work

You may often hear that it's important to build your network, but you may not know how to do that or why. A network of colleagues can be a source of support, strategies, job opportunities, helpful information, problem-solving, collaborations, and feedback that will help you work effectively and advance in the field if you wish. People in your networks help you—and you help them. Good networks include people inside and outside of your organization, people in your field and outside of it, and people at different levels of seniority. Plan to be open and friendly to lots of people to build a strong network.

1. **Approach building a network as a way to make lifelong relationships** with people who share your interests and goals, as well as with people who think and work differently than you.

2. **Talk to someone you trust outside of work, even outside your field, for an external opinion on how to build networks.** Ask them what social media they use (such as LinkedIn) for building networks and why. Consider any differences in their online network versus yours, and whether this is something you can adapt.

3. **Map your current network**, including people you network with who are junior to you, colleagues with you, and senior to you. Identify where you feel you would like more individuals and find them. Include people both within and outside your organization. Your professional network is likely much larger than your organization's network. Work on filling gaps by meeting people to strengthen your network.

4. **Invite a colleague to work on a project** with you to get to know them better.

5. **Offer something you may have to a colleague who is in need.** For example, if a colleague is interested in learning more about a topic, and you know someone who works in that area, offer to introduce them. Mutual sharing—of information, tips, opportunities, and support—strengthens networks faster than anything else.

6. **Identify people in your field who are doing interesting work** and invite them to coffee or a 15-minute phone conversation about their career path.

7. **Consider taking a professional development or certification class at work or in the community** to meet people in your line of work. Some companies or professional clubs have other non-work events, such as book club, environmental committee, or others that can also be places to meet and befriend colleagues.

8. **Commit to a goal of saying hello to one new person every day.** After you feel more comfortable saying hello, commit to starting a conversation, and then to asking someone to have coffee.

9. **Ask friendly colleagues if they'd be open to a networking lunch** periodically where you have a book club, review a recent article about your field, or discuss recent challenges. Many larger companies have network events for women, veterans, sports-related, LGBTQ, and other groups. Check out your company's website and ask around.

10. **Set up work-related meetings to get a chance to talk with people and ask them questions.** Sometimes it's easier when we can approach talking to someone as a work requirement instead of as our own initiative.

11. **Be aware that not everyone will like you, and that's okay.** There are some people you won't hit it off with. Others will resent you for your role or your decisions. Some people might be jerks. Be diplomatic and polite and keep moving forward.

12. **Identify the top publications in your field and read them.** Reach out to authors or people quoted in those publications to ask professional questions and potentially develop a relationship.

13. **Use social media that is typical for your field,** such as LinkedIn or Instagram. Always be professional. Consider creating a separate account for professional purposes.

14. **Identify other people at work who seem to have good networks** and build relationships with them. Ask them for tips on building networks.

15. **Attend conferences in your field** and make a point to introduce yourself to at least five people you don't know. You must put yourself out there to build networks. Prepare before networking events with a few questions or conversation starters. For example, start conversations by saying, "Tell me about what you do at your company."

See also: **Challenge 17: Understand your team—including your boss and your staff**

Challenge 68: Create a strong culture

Challenge 71: Integrating work and life

> **Take action: Research events that allow you to network with people you want to get to know better. What are 3-5 events you can attend in the next 6 months?**

Challenge 19.
Managing and organizing your time

Having a "system" for managing our time, priorities, and resources can make our work life so much easier—but for many of us, it's a challenge to set it up. If you struggle with organizing your time, here are options to help you figure it out.

1. **Consider professional training,** such as the "Getting Things Done" program that provides a system for organizing and completing tasks. (See the For further reading section)

2. **Make a list of everything that needs to be done.** If you're not a fan of paper, try virtual methods, such as OneNote or others. Consider all of the concrete activities, like reports you need to complete, as well as other activities that are your responsibility and take time. These might include staff management, mentoring/professional development, your own work, your own professional development. Identify how much time you'd like to spend on each task weekly, and how much you actually are spending. Identify anything that takes time that could be more effectively used, like chitchat.

3. **Rank items on your list in order of priority and commit to completing the first item on the list.** If you don't have enough time, consider that you may not be effectively prioritizing the time you have.

4. **Ask for help if you are not sure how work assignments should be prioritized.** Your boss should be able to help you understand their priorities so that you can make choices.

5. **If you have multiple bosses who each seek to monopolize your time,** ask to meet with all of them together to work out your

priorities across groups. Share your current list of activities and ask for feedback on how to ensure each group gets what it needs.

6. **Identify someone who seems very organized** and ask them how they stay focused on their priorities.

7. **Be aware that ways of keeping yourself organized may change over time.** Be flexible in adding and subtracting methods that can help you improve your overall time management strategies.

8. **Delegate or trade time-consuming activities** and those that detract from your effectiveness as a manager, such as scheduling meetings or creating agendas. Ask your staff to create meeting agendas.

9. **Talk to someone you trust outside of work** for an outside opinion.

10. **You may want to consider obtaining a coach or therapist** who can help you with time management and organization.

See also: **Challenge 3: Skills needed to be a good manager and leader**

   Challenge 13: Set professional goals

   Challenge 24: Manage and overcome overwhelm

Take action: Get it together! What are systems your colleagues or friends use to keep them organized? Try one new thing today.

Challenge 20.
How to lead a good meeting

Meetings can be challenging, both as someone running the meeting and as someone attending. It is possible to have useful meetings! It depends on how they're used and how everyone approaches them. Even if you are not in charge of the meeting, you can contribute to running better meetings.

1. **Ask for or provide the agenda for each meeting** if your position allows. If you're the boss, ask a staff member to be responsible for creating and distributing the agenda before the meeting.

2. **If you are running the meeting, use the first few minutes of each meeting to clarify the intent of the meeting**, ensure the right people are at the table to make decisions, and get updates on the task items from the last meeting. If you are not running the meeting, you can speak up and ask about these things yourself if it will help keep the meeting on track.

3. **If you are running the meeting, clarify that you expect people to participate in the meeting.** If they are too junior or too uncomfortable to actively participate, talk with them individually to identify any problems and help them feel more comfortable speaking up. Ask them questions in the meeting, and help them get more comfortable sharing their perspective. After the meeting, privately thank them for their perspective and encourage them to continue to share and bring value to the meeting.

4. **If many people are uncomfortable speaking up, go around the table and ask each person to provide one suggestion**, their opinion, etc., to move the conversation. If you are not leading the meeting, feel free to ask others what they think, such as by saying, "Mary, I'm wondering what you're thinking about this."

5. **Help keep people on topic and on track by gently redirecting to the topics on the agenda** and tabling other topics for the end if there's time or for the next meeting. It may be helpful to use a whiteboard or large notepad to list topics to come back to. Sometimes people refer to this as a "parking lot." You could say, for example, "That's a good idea, Sam. Let's put that on the parking lot and we'll get back to it once we finish these more pressing items" or "Thanks for all of your ideas. I want to make sure we stay focused on the problem, which is x. Who has a suggestion for how best to move forward?"

6. **Clearly document all decisions made in the meeting** including which person will be responsible to do what and by when. If you're the boss, you can ask someone to be responsible for this (the first few times, review and clarify with them so they can keep notes accurately and clearly to your expectations). Clarify expectations that people will give updates on items in their purview at each meeting and that you expect there to be progress between each meeting. Go over this list of action items at the end of the meeting to ensure everyone is on the same page. Ensure the list is sent out to everyone within a day after the meeting (it's not helpful if it comes right before the next meeting!).

7. **In the last few minutes of the meeting, make note of the time ("I notice we have about 10 minutes left in the meeting . . . "), and review what has been accomplished** and what next steps have been identified. Ensure these are written in the notes.

8. **If you are running the meeting, consider asking a junior person to take over running the meeting.** First talk with them about it and have them observe you run the meeting, and then have them take over running the meeting while you observe them. Finally, have them run the meeting during your absence with them reporting back to you what successes and challenges they experienced. You may want to groom this person by asking them to begin by taking over a specific portion of the meeting. This will allow you

to determine if you designated the person who can handle the meeting and will be respected by the attendees in future meetings.

9. **If there is a person in the meeting who is disruptive or who frequently gets the meeting off track,** talk with that person individually to request that they help the meetings move forward positively. You can always bring the meeting back to its purpose or agenda to help everyone get back on track.

10. **If there is a person who does not seem empowered by their boss to make decisions or contribute in the meeting,** talk to the person about how to improve the situation.

11. **Mix up the less exciting tasks such as note-taking or writing meeting minutes** so it's not always the same person who has to do this kind of work.

12. **Consider the culture of the meeting**—a tense environment in which everyone is on edge is not likely to bring out the best in the attendees. Cultivating an environment in which everyone is working together to solve problems you all have a stake in can help your meetings be more efficient.

13. **Reward efficiency.** If all items on the agenda have been discussed, ask for any additional items, and then let everyone leave early. Few people are disappointed at the prospect of ending a meeting early!

14. **Make a list of what meetings you attend.** Then consider the value of each meeting in terms of how helpful it is in achieving goals and priorities. Consider discussing with your staff or your boss to identify which meetings need to be improved and which you should no longer attend. If you determine you no longer will be attending a meeting, be sure to advise that meeting leader of your decision.

See also: **Challenge 9: When and how to obtain a mentor**

Challenge 18: Build allies and friendships at work

Challenge 19: Managing and organizing your time

Take action: What's your favorite tip from the above that you can begin using at your next meeting?

Challenge 21.
Office romance: Dos and Don'ts

Many people swear against office romances, while plenty of others meet their significant other in the workplace. Managers may have staff who start office romances, or they may find love at work themselves! Whatever you choose to do, be aware of the risks and be professional. Trust me, take the long view on this one.

1. **You generally get one chance for an office romance.** If you have more than one romance in the same office, you may not like how you will be perceived.

2. **Be aware of your organization's policies about office relationships,** and make sure your staff are aware. Many organizations forbid relationships between supervisors and supervisees; others require you to inform your supervisor of your relationship or sign a contract indicating you won't sue the organization if the relationship goes bad. Know the rules before you get started.

3. **Ask yourself if you would be willing to leave your job** if things became uncomfortable, such as if you break up.

4. **Never engage in public displays of affection at work** with a colleague and do not tolerate these as a manager. No lovebirds holding hands, no kissing, no nothing. It will not be helpful for you or your staff. If a couple's behavior is distracting, speak to them about it and ask them to knock it off.

5. **If you are friends with your colleagues on social media,** be wary of what you post about your office romance.

6. **Some people have very sensitive antennae to pick up on flirting.** If you or your staff are flirting with someone, be aware that others

may be noticing. For both you and your staff, It is best to keep flirting outside of work.

7. **If your organization is very conservative,** be especially careful of office romances, as they may be viewed more negatively than in less-conservative workplaces.

8. **If someone on your team is beginning an office romance,** have the difficult conversation with them and share that it may not be as secret as they think. Let them know relevant policies and ensure them you're available to discuss any concerns including if they decide to go public.

9. **Be aware of office politics or sensitivities related to LGBT issues if an office romance also means coming out.** (Hopefully this is a thing of the past.) If your organization or its employees are not supportive of you coming out, consider whether this is the right organization for you.

10. **If an office romance is going well and you or your staff would like to let people at work know about your relationship,** keep announcements low-key unless the announcement is an engagement. Be prepared to address any direct or indirect concerns about favoritism. As a manager, be prepared to shut down gossip.

11. **If you or someone on your team have a work-related break up, the goal is for everyone to stay professional at work.** If you or your staff member needs to take time off, or adjust work collaborations to stay professional, it's helpful to be flexible. Ensure other coworkers do not get pulled into drama or taking sides.

See also: **Challenge 11: Clarify your values**

Challenge 12: Learn how to have difficult conversations

Challenge 22: Learn to say no

Take action: Look up your office policies on office relationships so you're clear before any crushes start.

Challenge 22.
Learn how to say no

Saying no at work can be a tricky subject. Sometimes we want to say no because we don't think our team should be asked to do it, or it's just too much for our team. On the other hand, we are being paid to do a job and don't want to harm our professional relationships or reputation by saying no too often. Here are some suggestions for when and how to say no.

1. **If you think you might want to say no, ask for time to think about it.** A good phrase to use is, "When do you need an answer?"

2. **"No" might be appropriate if:** the work is outside of the scope of your division/team, you feel the work is unsafe or inappropriate, or you/your team will not be able to complete the work on time and with sufficient quality. Consider some professions/organizations have cultures that make it difficult to say no; chat with others if you feel like you *can't* say no.

3. **Consider whether you can offer an alternative instead of saying no.** For example, you could say, "We're happy to help with that project but our team is booked this week. Could we discuss it next week?" or "We're not able to do all of that now, but we could help with part of it. Would that work?"

4. **You can try to soften the no** by saying, "We appreciate the offer, but we can't" or "Thanks for thinking of us, but we are swamped" or "Sounds great, but we can't commit to the quality product you'll need right now."

5. **If you are asked at work to attend a non-work event for a staff member, such as a party, you don't need to provide an explanation.** In fact, it's often better to say no instead of explaining

("I have a date that night"; "My brother is in town"), because your explanations might lead the other person to feel it's okay to try to bargain with you ("Bring your brother!").

6. **If you have underlying resentments,** such as that you're not getting paid enough or you're overworked, deal with those directly so you aren't brusque when you're asked to do one more thing.

7. **If your difficulty saying no is affecting your work,** you can talk with your boss about helping you. If you have staff who are having trouble saying no, share this with them.

8. **If you say no to someone and they get angry, it doesn't necessarily mean you should have said yes.** It means there are issues on their side. Ideally the other person can have a reasonable conversation with you about the issue. If you think a staff person might get upset at your "no" or claim you're treating them unfairly, discuss with a colleague or with the Human Resources office if you have one.

9. **If you're not the right person for the job or if your team isn't available,** you could suggest someone else, especially if this is a good opportunity for a colleague.

10. **If there are certain activities you want to move off your team's responsibilities** permanently, have a discussion with your boss or the right person to make the transfer to someone else permanent. If someone asks you to do one of those tasks, you can say no or you could say, "Our team is no longer doing data entry. You could ask [other person who does data entry]."

11. **If a higher-up is asking you to do something illegal or unethical** or to continue a practice you feel is wrong, or if you feel unsafe saying no, attempt to get out of the situation and seek consultation from your boss, Human Resources (if available), or a trusted colleague. Ensure you don't put your staff in this position.

See also: **Challenge 7: Developing/determining your managing/leadership style**

Challenge 12: Learn how to have difficult conversations

Challenge 13: Set professional goals

Take action: What's something you need to say no to? What's stopping you? Knowing what you know now, how can you approach the situation differently the next time it comes up?

Challenge 23.
Be smart with social media at work

It's frustrating to walk up to your staff and find they are checking their phone. Then again, you probably are often checking your phone as well. . . . How do you balance your desire to check social media with your obligations at work?

1. **Learn your organization's policies about use of social media at work.** Many organizations track Internet usage on company computers. Do they allow you to check your personal email at work? Are employees allowed to send tweets or update Instagram while on the clock? All activity on company computers and phones is potentially subject to their review, so proceed accordingly.

2. **Ensure your staff understand the organization's social media policy.** You can also clarify that appearances are also important and being seen on social media leads to the assumption that they do not have enough work.

3. **Organizations may have concerns about how they are portrayed if you "tag" the organization or your coworkers,** or if you post information inconsistent with the organization's values. Ask if you are not sure about the policies.

4. **You may want to keep your social media separated into personal and professional venues;** for example, keep LinkedIn for professional contacts, and use Instagram only for personal use (and do not follow anyone you work with on your personal accounts). Note coworkers can find your social media profiles if your personal phone number is connected to your account.

5. **If you or your staff are on social media at work,** don't assume content is private or will be kept private, regardless of the privacy settings you chose.

6. **Never post a grievance about your workplace** unless you are a) out of all other options and b) okay with losing your job. If you have a concern about your workplace, take it to your boss or other appropriate person in the organization first, not to social media.

7. **Organizations may want you to post/repost certain information about company news and events.** Check regarding whether this is encouraged and decide if it's something you'd like to do from your professional accounts. There is no obligation for you to utilize your personal accounts to promote your organization's agenda unless you want to.

8. **Don't respond to any competitor or anyone posting negative information** or comments about the company. Let the company's public relations handle that. If you are concerned it is not being addressed, bring it up to your boss or a more appropriate person in your organization.

9. **When you change organizations, be sure to update your organizational affiliation** on your social media.

10. **When in doubt, look to your organization's policies or public relations** for guidance.

See also: **Challenge 12: Learn how to have difficult conversations**

Challenge 22: Learn how to say no

Challenge 56: Understanding hierarchy at work and when to go around it

Take action: Find and read your organization's policy on social media at work before you need to know.

Challenge 24.
Manage and overcome overwhelm

Sometimes it happens that we can't keep up! If everything keeps coming at us without a break, we can get completely overwhelmed. This is especially important as a manager and leader, when we are responsible for managing not only our own workload and priorities, but the workloads and priorities of our staff. Communicating your needs as a manager/leader and collaborating with others on how to ensure the most important things get done is a way through this challenge.

1. **Periodically during the day, stop and take a deep breath, stand, and stretch.** Take a short walk outside of your workspace if possible and check in with your staff. Build in regular breaks during the day to walk or meditate and clear your head. Even five minutes can be an important "reset" to help lower your stress.

2. **Talk with your boss to clarify their priorities for your tasks** so you and your staff can focus on them accordingly. Check in with your staff regarding their priorities to help them focus appropriately.

3. **Ask for more time if possible.** If enough time hasn't been allotted to finish a task or project, it's not surprising that you're feeling overwhelmed. It's more responsible to ask for more time than to deliver poor or sloppy work product because you didn't have enough time. When asking for more time, provide an update on the project's status, as well as the other things you're working on. This will help your boss understand your progress and your workload and help set reasonable expectations for a new deadline (or shifting your other responsibilities until the project at hand is complete).

4. **If you feel they will be open to it, share with your boss that you and your team are feeling overwhelmed** with the amount of work and ask for assistance in how to manage the workload, temporary assistance to complete tasks, or strategies to work more efficiently.

5. **Develop mantras that you can say to yourself, say to your team, or program in your phone** (such as setting affirmations using your phone alarms or an app such as MindJogger) to repeat during the day that will help you feel less frantic. For example, "You can do this!" or "One thing at a time" or "We can do this."

6. **Consider whether you or your team may be doing work that isn't yours.** Sometimes we pick up the work of others because we're good at it or because we are perfectionists. If you find yourself taking on tasks that aren't yours, figure out how to reallocate those tasks. In general, it's a good idea to have "the right tool for the job," which is matching the right person to the right task.

7. **If there are repetitive tasks or tasks that take a long time,** ask around to identify ways to do them more efficiently. Consider delegating to someone who is more efficient than you are in that particular task.

8. **Identify people who seem calm** and ask them what they do to stay calm in stressful situations. Thank your staff for being calm and steadfast.

9. **Consider starting a meditation or yoga practice** to manage your own stress.

10. **Consider whether you can take something off your to-do list, delay it, or delegate it.** You will still be responsible for completing the tasks, but at least you can focus on other things for a little while as someone else works through the details. Delegating also gives you the opportunity to help someone more junior and practice your mentoring skills.

11. **If you're in a workplace with constant chaos** (that you may have inherited from your predecessor), identify ways to reduce the chaos, such as streamlining processes or improving communication. Ask your staff to suggest ideas to reduce chaos as well.

12. **You may want to consider obtaining a coach** who can help you prioritize tasks and reduce your feelings of being overwhelmed.

See also: **Challenge 9: When and how to obtain a mentor**

                Challenge 13: Set professional goals

                Challenge 29: How to help staff stay motivated

                Challenge 65: Boss has unreasonable expectations

Take action: What's your favorite mantra to help keep you motivated? Write it down and consider sticking it on a Post-it note you can see each day.

Challenge 25.
Commit to continuous self-improvement

I believe life is about learning. As we take part in work, relationships, leisure, and all activities during our lives, we are also learning skills about strengthening our emotional and physical power, being authentic, negotiating effectively, and becoming better people. In your role as a manager and leader, it's important to commit to continuous self-improvement. Here are some ideas:

1. **Allow time for reflection.** It's easy to hit the ground running, but you want to make sure you're headed in the right direction! At least once a week, take some time to review what you've learned and ensure you're on the right track.

2. **Create an advisory board in your head**—or in real life—who can give you recommendations for what to learn or how to proceed. Sometimes I ask myself, "What would my advisory board recommend?" It's surprising to me that I often get a really good answer.

3. **You may want to keep a journal of your accomplishments**. This will be helpful to keep your resume up to date and also to discuss with your boss during your performance review.

4. **Get used to not knowing.** The more you advance, and truly the more you get older, you're more likely to not know all the information, not know the answer, or not know how the story will end. Be comfortable and embrace what you don't know. Consider it an opportunity to validate someone else's knowledge by asking them—they will appreciate it. Learn to enjoy the journey and learning as you go.

5. **Periodically reassess how far you've come.** You've grown so much since you were 15 years old! You've learned so much, even in the past year. Acknowledge and welcome the growth, and see that you're continuing to learn and grow.

6. **Learn how to learn faster.** Identify opportunities to learn quickly and practice applying those new skills. These can include reading summaries then applying the information, increasing your reading comprehension speed, or choosing to learn when you're waiting in line or otherwise not doing anything.

7. **Consider teaching others.** When you are teaching, you are constantly learning.

8. **Remember you will have content or technical skills** (such as finance or programming) as well as other "soft" skills, such as resilience, negotiation skills, networking skills, patience, and communication. Find opportunities to work on *all* the needed skills.

9. **How can you share your information with others?** Find people who are good at what you want to learn and offer to trade expertise.

10. **Consider podcasts as opportunities to learn** about new areas. Also books, newspapers, online media, Wikipedia, free online classes, online discussion forums . . . the list is endless!

11. **Ask people more senior to you what skills they wished they had honed,** and start working on improving those skills in yourself.

See also: **Challenge 13: Set professional goals**

Challenge 68: Create a strong culture

Challenge 83: Making sense of your career

Take action: Constantly challenge yourself to improve. What is one thing you can practice this week, this month, this year?

Part III.
Staff Development

Challenge 26.
Hiring strong staff

The best managers surround themselves with capable, competent people who soak up feedback, know when to ask questions, and reliably perform at the highest levels. How do you get great staff? Hire great staff!

1. **Many times, people think the most important aspect of hiring is finding someone who can do technical skills, but often that's only a baseline.** Often characteristics such as friendliness, the ability to work well in teams, persistence, humor, or striving for excellence are more important indicators of success. One of my colleagues used to say, "I can teach them how to do the job, but if they are adults who don't listen or can't get along, there's not much I can do to help them!"

2. **It's important to have a good idea of what you are looking for in the position.** Considering technical proficiency as a given, are you looking for someone who can pull together the team, start new areas of inquiry, or plan well? Or are you looking for someone with connections or experience in the industry? Or would you consider a candidate with less technical experience but who seems trainable and is a good team player?

3. **You may want to discuss with colleagues or your team what kind of person the position needs and what skills would be helpful.** Make a checklist if needed so you remember this information in the interview or while discussing it with the hiring team.

4. **Consider whether you would like experience vs. raw talent.** Both of these can bring strengths to your team: Individuals with experience are likely to be less reactive and have a broader base of knowledge but may be less willing to take direction. Raw talent

may have brains and energy but be more challenging to focus and corral.

5. **Hire people who are better than you.** Many leaders and managers worry their proteges might outshine them, so they hire less capable staff who are less threatening. This is a mistake! The best people will rise to the top anyway, and your staff keeping you on your toes isn't the worst thing. Plus, it's wonderful to be a part of a superstar's meteoric rise (and you get the reflected glory because you were smart enough to hire them). Similarly, find staff who complement your weaker areas, whether they can support you in technical skills, organization, warmth, or other expertise.

6. **Consider who should be included in interviewing a candidate,** and who gets to make the decision. Including all staff in interviewing a candidate can provide the false sense to staff that they all have equal weight in the decision. It also presents to the candidate that decisions are made by a group rather than by the manager.

7. **If your boss is pushing a candidate you don't prefer,** you can have the conversation regarding what the team needs and who you think would be best. Be diplomatic and not too harsh about the boss's preferred candidate, because you might get stuck with them anyway. These things aren't always fair.

8. **If you have staff you inherited who are not great, help them become great.** First you want to help those who are not performing at the minimum standard improve skills or move on to find something more appropriate. Then work on helping the good staff become great by motivating them, helping them learn and grow, and praising their success.

9. **Learn how to interview candidates well.** Some organizations have structured interview questions, but most leave managers on their own to improvise. Don't ask easy questions (e.g., "Do you know how to x?"); instead ask about their ability to think and make decisions and collaborate. Ask about challenging situations, a time they

struggled with a coworker or boss, and how they would go about approaching a sample realistic task from work. Some managers even give a written prompt for a simulated work task and have the candidate spend 15-30 minutes preparing a written answer. Also probe for their level of self-awareness, including what they need from a boss, and how they need to be successful. The content of their answers is important, but so is their communication style, ease in speaking with you, and awareness of social cues.

10. **Hire for diversity—yes, ethnic/racial and gender diversity—but also diversity of thought, experience, and approach.** Allow the new hire to retain the uniqueness that you hired them for.

11. **Check references, and don't ask only easy questions.** There are some legal limits on what questions you can ask a reference; for example, you can't ask about personal demographic information such as race, religion, pregnancy status, or disability status. You can, however, ask if the employer would hire the candidate again, what the candidate's strengths and weaknesses are, how the candidate got along with colleagues, what it's like to work with the candidate, and what the candidate needs to be most successful. Document everything.

12. **Once you find the right person for the job, help them hit the ground running!** Announce their arrival as broadly as appropriate, make sure they have an orientation to your department (in addition to any orientation your organization might provide), and identify who they can go to with questions. Check in with them and with your other staff frequently at first to see how it's going and to ensure the new person is successful.

See also: **Challenge 3: Skills needed to be a good manager and leader**

                Challenge 15: Starting a new job as a manager or leader

                Challenge 22: Learn how to say no

Take action: What are you looking for in staff you hire? How can you ensure you hire staff with those qualities?

Challenge 27.
Developing and retaining strong staff

Most people want to learn and grow. As a manager and leader, you can help your employees with professional development opportunities they might not have considered. Employees understand that being offered professional development opportunities means that you are investing in their careers beyond just what they're doing for you currently; this can improve morale and their loyalty to you.

1. **Tell your staff that you value professional development.** Maximize learning opportunities by requesting or requiring all staff who obtain company-funded training share what they learned with others on the team formally or informally. This doubles as a professional development opportunity in synthesizing and presenting to teams!

2. **Model your values of professional development and the importance of lifelong learning.** Share what you learn when you go to training or conferences, send around information from professional associations, and bring up current events in your field during staff meetings so everyone learns all the time.

3. **Ask lots of questions** to help your team start working through a project or tackle a conundrum. Sometimes we get stuck thinking that because we are the manager or leader that we have to know everything. But it's often better for everyone involved if the boss is asking questions and helping staff figure out things on their own, rather than directing them or micromanaging. By asking questions for your team to work out an answer to, you can understand their thinking processes and provide guidance about inaccurate

assumptions or more effective strategies. You might even learn something!

4. **Train staff to bring you solutions, not problems.** If your staff think you're there to solve their problems for them, they will bring you problems. Teach them to bring you solutions when they bring you challenges. This will create opportunities for providing feedback on their problem solving strategies.

5. **Provide professional development opportunities in your day-to-day activities.** Here are some examples: delegate a small part of a project or a whole project to a staff member; ask a staff member to report on some component of their work at a small meeting (they can prepare the material and review it with you to get feedback before the meeting); invite a staff member to attend a higher-level meeting to learn more about organizational context (be sure to prepare them for the meeting, ask what they learned, and request they report back to their colleagues in a meeting about their experience).

6. **Find out what training funds or tuition reimbursement may be provided to employees** and whether the organization supports paid time to attend training. Consider professional development in technical areas of your field (e.g., finance, law) and also in soft skills like written communication, leadership, and public speaking. Share this information with your staff and encourage them to take advantage of the opportunities.

7. **Assist staff in identifying their mentoring needs** and provide support around these needs, whether technical or softer skills such as negotiation, communication, or process improvement. For specific technical needs, invite a colleague from another department in your organization to present to your staff and engage them in a discussion about the topic. You can offer to return the favor to their department, possibly including one of your staff as an additional professional development opportunity.

8. **Consider a book club/journal club.** You and your staff might be interested in reading an article or book together or engaging in regular discussion of current events. If so, tap staff members to identify date/time of conversations, distribute the article/book, and facilitate the meeting. You can initially facilitate the meetings to show them how. Use the meetings, however, as an opportunity for others to step up and take responsibility for keeping the meetings going.

9. **Let them make mistakes.** You can't save staff from ever making mistakes, and sometimes you have to let them fail. You can assist them in identifying what went wrong, how to do it differently, and how to manage failure.

10. **Professional associations and federal agencies may have materials or training** available to your staff for them to access individually or as a team training, depending on your field.

11. **Give stretch assignments,** which are those that are developmentally challenging for a person and require them to work beyond their current skills, but not so far that they feel incompetent and fail. We may be tempted to give every assignment to the person who is best at it, but then others don't get a chance to learn! Consider who is a good fit for the assignment and how you can support them in their learning process (while still being successful with the assignment).

12. **Check in regularly.** Weekly scheduled supervision or 1:1's helps staff feel safe and consistent so that you're not only talking to them when you need to give them critical feedback. Regular meetings allow you to develop a relationship, get updates on tasks, reassess needs, and answer questions.

13. **Mentors help their staff learn and grow; sponsors actively advocate for their staff and open doors to help them become even more successful.** Introduce your staff to the right content experts, role models, and prospective mentors. Encourage them to build relationships widely and, of course, to pay it forward.

14. **Help your staff navigate office politics.** The best content knowledge won't help someone with politics, and junior staff often need help recognizing politics and learning how to respond in a savvy manner. You can bring some political challenges (possibly de-identified) to the team to discuss as a group, or role play with an employee about a challenge they are having. Reinforce that politics are a reality, not an option, and that everyone can choose how to respond to these (sometimes unpleasant) realities.

15. **Introduce new responsibilities piece by piece,** such as having someone observe the process, then become a part of the team that completes it, and finally leading the team to complete the process. Provide opportunities for staff to ask questions and provide feedback.

16. **Provide staff with feedback frequently.** Your best staff will be hungry for feedback because they want to keep improving. Be specific; not, "This report looks great," but rather, "I like how you made your three main points clearly and succinctly." Provide suggestions for improvement, such as, "If you were to do this again, I suggest you could xxx," or "This is great, and to make it even more effective, you could yyy."

17. **Continually provide honest praise**—look for good things your staff are doing and let them know how much you appreciate them.

18. **Ensure staff are engaged and not bored.** Keeping them busy with projects to complete helps them stay focused on their work.

19. **Help your staff advocate for themselves.** If you see it's time for your staff to get a raise or promotion, help them identify how and advocate with them.

See also: **Challenge 12: Learn how to have difficult conversations**

Challenge 26: Hiring strong staff

Challenge 68: Create a strong culture

Take action: What professional development was most helpful for you? How can you give that to your staff?

Challenge 28.
Addressing cultural differences

Workplaces can be like families, where there is support for each other. They can also be like families in that there are lots of differences and people don't always get along. Work, however, is a place where it's important to get along. You don't have to like everyone, but you do have to be respectful and diplomatic and work together. If you see yourself on the management track, this is especially important.

1. **Do what you can to create a culture of diversity and inclusion** by being respectful to everyone and not engaging in or tolerating disrespectful behavior.

2. **Invite presenters from multiple cultures** represented in your group to moderate a discussion about cultural differences.

3. **Check with your organization's diversity office or diversity-focused groups in your profession.** Identify how you and your team could get involved and learn.

4. **Check in with team members individually and regularly** about how any diversity issues in the office may be affecting them and find out how you can help.

5. **Mentor others more junior than you,** especially groups that are under-represented in senior leadership. You always have something to offer, even if only support.

6. **Use pronouns and names that individuals request.**

7. **Understand that some people may not intend to be disrespectful and may just lack awareness or be culturally insensitive.** This doesn't mean that their behavior is acceptable; only that it's

important not to assume negative intent. If someone is disrespectful to you or others, make it a priority to talk with them about it, and escalate if needed.

8. **Be aware that there are often stark differences by seniority and tenure at organizations.** Try to assume positive intent. For example, if you keep receiving menial assignments, instead of assuming it's because you're the youngest person, talk to your boss about your ability to do more challenging work. Someone has to do the menial work, though, and if you're the most junior, it might be you until someone more junior is hired or until you move up.

9. **Keep clear boundaries about violations, and also choose your battles.** Sometimes people say stupid or hurtful things, including ageist comments about Millennials and other younger or older team members. This is counterproductive.

10. **Although it's important to speak your mind, sometimes it's more appropriate to observe the situation and ask questions or speak up later.** For example, if there is a very senior meeting with your boss, your boss's boss, and that person's boss too, that might not be the best time to ask a question or provide an insight unless specifically requested. There are political issues at play that you might not see. Instead, observe carefully and ask your boss questions privately later.

11. **Be open to feedback** on your own behavior if you are unintentionally disrespectful to someone.

12. **Speak with a mentor or trusted colleague** if you have concerns about the organization's approach to diversity.

See also: **Challenge 12: Learn how to have difficult conversations**

Challenge 24: Manage and overcome overwhelm

Challenge 42: Staff are aggressive, racist, sexist, homophobic, or hostile

Take action: Consider the ways in which each of your colleagues and staff brings a unique strength or perspective to work. Everyone has something unique to offer.

Challenge 29.
How to help staff stay motivated

"If you want to build a ship, don't drum up people to gather wood, divide the work, and give orders. Instead, teach them to yearn for the vast and endless sea." Motivating people, as author of The Little Prince Antoine de Saint-Exupery noted, can be an indirect and challenging endeavor. Nevertheless, staff will perform much better and be more satisfied when they are motivated.

1. **Humor can help put things in perspective, bring people together, relieve stress, increase engagement, improve morale, and increase creativity.** Using positive humor—no put-downs of anyone—can be as simple as starting a meeting by saying, "Does anyone have a good clean joke?"

2. **Expressing appreciation for the work of your staff can work wonders.** Letting people know you see that they are working hard, pushing themselves, helping others, or otherwise doing a great job can motivate staff to persevere through difficult times. Be as specific as possible in describing exactly what they did and why it was so wonderful. You can also mix it up by letting people know individually verbally, writing a note, and sharing appreciation in a larger group. Praise the effort, the result, the creativity, the persistence, or whatever they are doing well. Note progress when you see it and keep encouraging them to get even better.

3. **Help staff set and strive toward goals.** Help them identify what they want to learn (or if they're not clear on what they want to learn, what you think they *need* to learn to be successful). Find something they can get motivated about and help them take steps forward.

4. **Set an example.** Sometimes it's helpful to talk through steps out loud as you're doing them so the other person can understand your thought process. Saying, "Wow. This is so frustrating. I wonder what I could do differently to make this work better," is empowering to junior people because they see how to keep going despite feeling frustrated, and how to think through problems without losing motivation.

5. **Help staff see there's a connection between targeted hard work and success.** Check to see if they are working effectively—not working hard only for the sake of working hard—so their efforts are targeted toward the goals they want to achieve.

6. **Notice discouragement and pay attention to negative talk.** If you have staff who say, "I'm not really good at this," or "I don't know where to start," or "I don't know what to do," start asking questions. In a supportive way, you can find out what they need and help think through the task at hand. Ensure staff understand they can let you know if they're struggling without being punished or feeling like this will be a strike against them. And notice when they're struggling and offer to help.

7. **Help staff understand the steps in sequence of operations** and implications of their actions. It's hard for junior people to see the big picture sometimes in complicated processes such as what all the steps in the process are and who handles the step before their work and the step after it. Helping them understand the big picture can improve their skills, help build their network, and also reduce isolation since they understand more that they are part of a larger team.

8. **Ensure staff have the proper training and the right tools for the job.** Help them understand what skills and tools are needed and help them get the right ones.

9. **Protect them from bullying and harassment from others.** Be fiercely protective of your staff. If someone is harassing staff or bullying your staff—even if they made a mistake—talk with your

staff and the bully about what is going on and help resolve the situation.

10. **Help staff learn and grow.** When frustrating things happen, reassure staff that everyone makes mistakes and that our obligation is to learn from them. Ask them to tell you the steps they took to solve a problem, what their assumptions were, and how they made decisions. You can then ask them questions that challenge their observations, assumptions, or decisions. Ask questions to help them identify where things went wrong and how to do things better next time.

See also: **Challenge 11: Clarify your values**

Challenge 12: Learn how to have difficult conversations

Challenge 13: Set professional goals

Take action: What is the "ship" you and your team are building? How can you help motivate them to get excited about that?

Challenge 30.
Delegating work

A big challenge many new leaders and managers have is learning to delegate work to others and following up on it. Follow these suggestions, practice, and become a master delegator.

1. **Start small.** It's hard to let go of big tasks when you're responsible for their completion. Delegate small items first. Check back in to ensure they are being completed appropriately. And give clear, precise feedback until the work is done to your standards.

2. **Clarify your expectations.** This is often a communication challenge, especially if you are not sure what you want. For more junior/less experienced staff, be very concrete, including seemingly simplistic details (for example, the font, the margins, etc.). You may even want to outline what you're looking for in writing so they can complete the outline. For more experienced staff, you can give more general expectations, such as "I want a 2-page report that will explain our activities over the past year," and they can figure out the steps to get what you're looking for.

3. **Give a timeline.** Let your staff know when you expect them to have completed part or all of the project and let them know how to get it to you. For example, you could say, "I'd like to see an outline of the report on Friday, with the final report a week from Friday. Please email me the draft and free up a half hour on Friday for us to review the outline."

4. **Follow up to ensure tasks are completed correctly.** You might want to schedule a halfway point check-in so you can see progress. If progress hasn't been made or is not what you're looking for, clarify your expectations.

5. **Praise what your staff did well and provide corrections and direction in a positive way.** Most people are trying to do what you're asking them to do, and it's often best to be positive when you know someone is trying. If you feel like someone isn't giving you their best work or is blowing you off, ask them about it instead of responding harshly. You could say, "I've seen your completed work with much more detail and accuracy than this. Was there something going on this week that you couldn't give this your usual high level of attention?" Give them a chance to explain.

6. **If tasks are not done how you want them, clarify what you're looking for and ask the person to give it another try.** You may want to suggest a more senior person review the junior person's work product and provide feedback so they can revise before they send it to you.

7. **Clarify your priorities.** Staff who are completing multiple tasks may understandably get confused when they're asked to do many things at once. Let them know what deadlines you have and how to prioritize tasks. Let them know they can check in with you if they have any questions.

8. **Teach new skills.** You can't expect your staff to know everything you do, and you might need to teach them or at least help them learn. If it becomes clear someone doesn't know how to do something, either show them or direct them to a resource or peer so they can learn. Many companies offer training in skills such as managing spreadsheets and basic programming; there are also videos online that individuals can watch and then ask you questions about. Build time into your request if the person needs training or coaching on a new skill.

9. **Play to your staff's strengths and give learning opportunities depending on the urgency of the project.** Ideally, there is plenty of time for everything to be a learning opportunity with lots of attention from you to ensure they get it right. In reality, however, we often don't have time to do as much training and mentoring as

we'd like. When there's an urgent task, give it to the person who can get it done quickly and correctly. Save learning opportunities for times when you have more flexibility.

10. **Ask staff for feedback.** The goal is to have a smooth process where you delegate tasks with clear expectations and timelines, and the staff can address your requests accurately and timely. If you're not providing enough information to them, or they feel confused by what you're asking for, work to clarify and provide more support. If their feedback is negative, this will give you options for how to improve.

See also: **Challenge 14: Start seeing yourself as a manager/ leader**

Challenge 16: Understanding your organization and its mission

Challenge 17: Understanding your team–including your boss and your staff

Take action: What concerns you about delegating work? How can you best address that concern?

Challenge 31.
Supervising someone older than you

I have had the exciting and intimidating experience of supervising people older than me. It is definitely challenging to be in charge of a team at 25 years old when everyone else on the team is in their 30s and 40s. As a Millennial manager or leader, you are likely to run into this issue. A lot. Read on . . .

1. **Communicate effectively, which includes both speaking AND listening.** Many times, we speak too much because we want others to understand how capable we are. Unfortunately, this can result in staff of any age feeling their ideas and perspectives are being dismissed, especially older staff who bring years of experience. Resources on listening are available in the For further reading section.

2. **Leverage the strengths of your team.** Your older staff have more experience than you, as well as unique talents and strengths. Find a way to identify what they uniquely bring to the table, recognize their gifts, and incorporate their strengths into the conversation.

3. **Limit age-related statements and self-deprecating humor among your team.** Become aware of how others will react to statements like, "I'm old enough to be your mother," or "I wasn't born when 9/11 happened." Although these statements may be entirely accurate, even when staff are joking it can rub people the wrong way unnecessarily.

4. **Put your team and the mission first.** Although it might feel important to have the right title, the larger office, or to speak up first in the meeting, it may be more impactful to identify

what's best for the team and the mission. Your strength will be noticed.

5. **Consider how to address questions or comments about your age or appearance.** Although people aren't supposed to ask these questions, someone will inevitably ask you how old you are or if you remember cultural events that happened before you were born. Consider how you feel about the questions, and make sure you have a prepared answer or at least a playful deflection. If you feel such questions might throw you off guard, practice with a friend or in front of a mirror so you can answer nonchalantly or at least without frustration or anger. I once had an employee reply angrily to a request, "I'm old enough to be your mother!" Thankfully my response was ready: "It's really not appropriate for *either* of us to talk about age in the workplace."

6. **Aim for respect, not for being liked.** This is a developmental task for most of us in our 30s, but as a manager or leader supervising older staff, it's critical. Regardless of your age, if you let your staff walk all over you, they will no longer respect you. Stay tough and hold your ground.

7. **Consider how you present to others.** One day when I was rushing around trying to put out another fire, my boss stopped me in the hallway and said, "When you act anxious, they will feel anxious. When you act calm, they will feel calm." #truth. This has been a valuable lesson to me as a manager. Note that it really doesn't matter WHY you feel anxious.

8. **Consider whether it would be worthwhile to modify your hair, piercings, tattoo visibility, or wardrobe.** I'm not suggesting you totally change your entire appearance, but sometimes minor adjustments can be effective in changing perspectives while still feeling authentic to you.

9. **Remember your value.** Don't let anyone (anywhere) diminish your sense of self-worth. You are in this role because someone

believes in you. Do your thing, seek consultation when needed, and know that you're in control.

10. **Teach your staff *and* learn from them.** We all have something to learn. For everything you bring to the table in energy, innovation, or whatever your unique superpowers, your staff have experience, political savvy, knowledge of others, and so much more to teach you.

11. **When you feel self-doubt, recall other times where you started something ambitious and completed it**—whether high school sports, an art project, college, basic military training, or something else. Stay focused, open to learning, authentic, and diplomatic, and things will be okay.

See also: Challenge 12: Learn how to have difficult conversations

Challenge 68: Create a strong culture

> **Take action: Whether the friction comes from your side or their side, it still needs to be addressed. What kind of conversation can you have—with the staff member, with a colleague, with your boss, or with a coach/mentor—that can help you gain insight?**

Challenge 32.
Being a good mentor

Many Millennials may think they're too young or too inexperienced to mentor someone else. That's a myth! Everyone has something to offer, including people junior to you, people at your level of seniority, and people senior to you. By virtue of having reached your age and position, you know stuff that others can benefit from.

1. **Lift as you climb.** In some organizations, knowledge is used as power and doled out only to certain people viewed as having earned it. Be generous with your knowledge and help people when you can.

2. **Be honest and clear in your availability and boundaries regarding your areas of expertise, time, availability, and style.** Give honest feedback to your mentee, including if they are not holding up their side of mentoring, such as following up or scheduling meetings.

3. **Deliver what you promise.** Most mentees want regular check-ins. When you first start a mentoring relationship, ask them to share what they are looking for and what they expect. Then you can both decide how you'd like to set up the relationship. For example, do you meet monthly in your office, or is the mentee free to text you any concerns or questions at any time?

4. **Conduct an informal needs assessment with your mentee so you both can clarify what the mentee is looking for.** This can help you understand not only the stated goal (I want a job in marketing), but the other skills that may be needed (increase communication skills, political savvy, and network). Once you know what is needed, you can work together to set goals.

5. **Recognize your limitations** and refer your mentee to others as needed for specific topics, unique opportunities, or if you have a conflict of interest in the topic. This expands your own and your mentees' networks.

6. **Accept the responsibility of being a mentor.** It is an important responsibility to help shape someone's career and to develop them as a person! You are responsible for holding your mentees accountable to make sure that meetings happen, actions are completed, and targets are reached. Ensure you don't take on more responsibility than you can manage.

7. **Advocate for and promote your mentee.** Mention to interested others how wonderful your mentee is, how hard they've been working, what they've achieved, or how proud of them you are. When your mentee's name comes up, make sure to put in a good word.

8. **Mentors should be role models.** Assume your mentees and staff are observing you at work, because they are! Share the rewards and enthusiasm about work and be frank about your frustrations. Focus on both technical skills and "real life," such as what a week is typically like, how you balance work and life, or how you approach conferences. Communicate the importance of mentoring and your hope that your mentees will also mentor others.

9. **Let them make their own decisions.** Although you may think you know more about everything (!), telling them what to do will deprive them of the opportunity to learn. Focus on asking questions and provide feedback on their assumptions, thought processes, and strategies rather than directing them what to do.

10. **If you need to end a mentoring relationship, be honest and clear about why and when and how.** I typically let my mentees know I'm available to them for the rest of our careers, but occasionally I need to end a mentoring relationship because the mentee isn't using our time well, is chronically unprepared, or I have exhausted what I have to give them. When this happens, I recommend sharing

this information with them kindly, suggesting other mentors and possibly encouraging them to contact you if circumstances change.

11. **Enjoy being a mentor!** Delight in watching your mentees learn and grow and increase their confidence. You are making a positive difference in the world by contributing to another person's success and development.

See also: **Challenge 9: When and how to obtain a mentor**

Challenge 12: Learn how to have difficult conversations

Challenge 68: Create a strong culture

Take action: Identify ways in which your knowledge, skills, or experience can help someone else. Keep this in mind for when an opportunity arises.

Part IV.
Staff challenges

Challenge 33.
Your staff are disrespectful to each other

Some offices have friendly environments in which everyone jokes around; other times, however, environments can be toxic. If your staff are disrespectful to each other, it can negatively affect both morale and productivity. As the boss, it's your responsibility to ensure a respectful and civil work environment.

1. **Recognize disrespectful behavior in the workplace.** It can include snide comments, raised voices or name-calling, physical fighting, or undermining. Work-based disrespectful behavior can lead to lost productivity and increased stress, as well as have a negative impact on the workplace environment and employee turnover.

2. **Stay calm.** Escalating when you see disrespectful behavior will not help, it will only make you look like you are out of control.

3. **Clarify your expectations for respectful communication to your team.** Make it clear that disrespect to anyone will not be tolerated.

4. **Aggression should not be tolerated.** This includes yelling, cursing, name-calling, making threats in general or threats specifically about using weapons. Depending on your company's resources, you may wish to notify building security or suspend the employee until they have received an evaluation. You should work with your Human Resources office (if you have one) to contact local law enforcement and file a report if the employee's behavior violates the law.

5. **Ensure that you are not inadvertently being disrespectful.** If you realize you have been, apologize and pledge to do better.

6. **Ask a colleague for feedback** about your team's respectful attitudes toward each other. Let your colleague know you are working on this with your team and would appreciate hearing about any observations or concerns.

7. **Talk individually with a few staff who are well respected by others** to ask if they have noticed a problem and if so, how they suggest you should deal with it. Reiterate your expectations to them so they can share them with their colleagues.

8. **Schedule periodic "check-in" meetings** about respectful conversations and give the staff an opportunity to discuss what has improved and what has not improved. Reinforce accountability and learning.

9. **Consider whether what you are observing is healthy tension**, in which two groups have opposing goals (e.g., one group needs to get documents submitted fast and another group is responsible for checking all details for accuracy). Healthy tension should still be respectful. Bring both teams together to voice their concerns and improve processes so that both groups can be more successful together, and make it clear that unprofessional behavior will not be tolerated.

10. **Be sure everyone knows what respect and disrespect looks like.** Ask individuals to share with you examples of respectful and disrespectful reactions from coworkers. Discuss with your team and identify together how the team would like to move forward.

11. **Always document disrespectful interactions with employees** in case you need them to provide counseling, performance feedback, or a written warning.

12. **This is an excellent opportunity to make this a learning experience** for your staff and to model appropriate behavior. Discuss difficult items forthrightly, be compassionate, listen, and move forward.

13. **You may need to provide written feedback and clarification of expectations** as part of a formal performance improvement plan for the employee. If your organization has a Human Resources office, you will want to involve them in the process.

14. **You may want to consider obtaining a coach or mediator** who can help you or your team through this challenge. If your organization has a Human Resources office, they may be able to advise or help.

See also: **Challenge 3: Skills needed to be a good manager and leader**

                Challenge 11: Clarify your values

                Challenge 47: Need to give difficult feedback to staff

Take action: Periodically assess your office climate for mutual respect. Ask your staff and colleagues about how much they feel respected. The answers may surprise you!

Challenge 34.
Your staff are disrespectful to you

Staff being disrespectful to each other is a challenge; when they are disrespectful to you—openly challenging your authority, dismissing you, or not following instructions—you have a bigger problem on your hands. It's important to take care of this situation immediately so it doesn't affect the morale of everyone on your team.

1. **Know how disrespect toward a boss looks different than disrespect to colleagues.** Some examples of this are: when an employee deliberately slows work; submits bad-faith complaints; or manipulation, such as saying negative untrue things about their bosses.

2. **You may want to consider obtaining a coach, mediator, or assistance from Human Resources** who can help you or your team through this challenge. Every manager experiences situations like this, and the use of HR and the support of your senior team is hugely helpful in navigating these challenges. If you feel supported, you will be able to handle this more successfully. If you're not supported, it may become clear that you need to move on from the company. In general, Human Resources and/or your superiors should be notified and involved every step of the way.

3. **Clarify your expectations for respectful communication to your team.** Make it clear that disrespect to anyone will not be tolerated.

4. **Identify whether it is one person who is disrespectful to you,** one person who is disrespectful to everyone, or if there is a general environment of disrespect. If it's one person, talk with them directly and ask them to stop. If it is a broader issue, talk with an opinion leader in the group who is tactful and mature to

determine whether other people are bothered by the environment of disrespect.

5. **Ensure that you are not inadvertently being disrespectful.** If you realize you have been, apologize and pledge to do better.

6. **Discuss standards for professionalism, civility, and respect directly with your supervisee during onboarding and document that you have done so.** This will give you strong footing if someone becomes disrespectful later on. These standards should be described in the employee handbook or company policies. Managers, leaders, and supervisors should be trained to uphold standards of professionalism, which includes taking responsibility for how we present ourselves to others.

7. **Document disrespectful interactions** with employees in case you need them to provide counseling, performance feedback, or a written warning. If you already have weekly meetings and document your discussions, that makes it easier to have these conversations.

8. **Be direct when you talk with the employee** about their behavior. Be respectful, explain you are concerned about their behavior and the way they treat you, review the events you documented, and clarify that this behavior is unacceptable.

9. **Aggression should not be tolerated.** This includes yelling, cursing, name-calling, making threats in general or threats specifically about using weapons. Depending on your company's resources, you may wish to notify building security or suspend the employee until they have received an evaluation. You should work with your human resources office (if you have one) to contact local law enforcement and file a report if the employee's behavior violates the law.

10. **This is an excellent opportunity to make this a learning experience** for your staff and to model appropriate behavior. Discuss difficult items forthrightly, be compassionate, listen,

and move forward. Do not, however, discuss the specifics of the problem with staff, such as identifying who the person is. Your employees see and hear a lot, and likely know who it is. But talking about it with them breaches confidentiality and employment laws.

11. **You may need to provide written feedback and clarification of expectations** as part of a formal performance improvement plan for the employee. If your organization has a Human Resources office, you will want to involve them in the process.

See also: **Challenge 14: Start seeing yourself as a manager/ leader**

                Challenge 31: Supervising someone older than you

                Challenge 47: Need to give difficult feedback to staff

Take action: Disrespect should not be tolerated. Identify how you want to proceed, including consulting with someone else about your response, discussing with a friend, or responding directly to the individual.

Challenge 35.
Staff do not complete work

Part of your job as a manager is to ensure your staff get things done. If they're not completing their work, that reflects poorly on you. Having these difficult conversations with employees can be challenging, and your tone and professionalism will be extremely important.

1. **Discuss expectations for completing work with your supervisee during onboarding and document that you have done so.** This will give you strong footing if someone has challenges later on.

2. **Ask your staff to make a list of everything on their plate** so that you can understand where they are prioritizing this work. I did this once with a staff member and found out she was prioritizing work her colleagues gave her over work her boss gave her.

3. **Ensure staff understand exactly what is required and in what time frame.** Provide samples, templates, or checklists if possible.

4. **Encourage staff to check in with you with any problems.** Make sure that when they do, you respond in a way that encourages them to continue to bring problems to you. Be available to them, listen, respond, and do not chastise. At the same time, provide enough support to encourage them to learn to solve problems themselves.

5. **It is possible there are outside issues that are leading your staff to be unmotivated, oppositional, or otherwise not doing their best.** Talk with several key staff members to ask for their help understanding what else might be affecting the team.

6. **Consider if morale is an issue.** If so, check out *Challenge 38. Low staff morale.*

7. **It's possible the work has so many steps that rely on other people outside your office that it's nearly impossible to complete everything on time.** Ask key staff to walk you through the steps to completing the work and let you know where things get stuck. Some process improvement techniques or conversations with other teams can help you work out the kinks. It's also possible the staff don't know all the steps, which presents another kind of learning opportunity.

8. **After you've provided the expectations, ask your staff to recap so you are sure they've understood the priorities.** If they repeat back incomplete or inaccurate instructions, correct the error and ask them to repeat back again.

9. **Ask your staff to complete a time chart to identify how they are spending their time at work,** rounded to nearest 30 minutes or so. That will give you an idea of which projects are taking the right amount of time, too little (which means quality may suffer), or too much (which means the staff don't understand the assignment or may be inefficient). This is a temporary solution, as it takes time for staff to complete the chart.

10. **Clarify that your staff is ultimately responsible for getting the work done, even if other people are involved.** Let them know that if they have problems with other team members, they have the authority to address the problems or bring them to you to discuss.

11. **Schedule periodic "check-in" meetings** before the deadline to provide feedback and give the staff an opportunity to improve the work before the actual deadline. Reinforce accountability and learning.

12. **Consider joining your staff on a site visit or at another activity to see how the work proceeds.** Let them know you want to see how things are going, and then ask them their perspective of how typical/atypical that event was, what went well/not well, and then offer feedback.

13. **This is an excellent opportunity to make this a learning experience** for your staff and to model appropriate behavior. Ensure your strategies for getting things done are effective; otherwise, seek help yourself so you can model learning and growing. Discuss difficult items forthrightly, be compassionate, listen, and move forward.

14. **You may need to provide written feedback and clarification of expectations** as part of a formal performance improvement plan for the employee. If your organization has a Human Resources office, they may be able to provide assistance.

See also: **Challenge 29: How to help staff stay motivated**

Challenge 32: Being a good mentor

Challenge 47: Need to give difficult feedback to staff

Challenge 68: Create a strong culture

Take action: What would happen to your job if you didn't complete your work? Hmmm . . . Something to think about!

Challenge 36.
Staff complete work with low quality

Perhaps the work gets done, but it is of such low quality as to be unusable. Instead of redoing the work yourself, here are some suggestions that can help you fix this problem.

1. **State your expectations clearly at the beginning of the project,** including the purpose of the assignment, what you expect will be completed, and when it is due.

2. **After you've provided the expectations, ask your staff to repeat the instructions back to you so you are sure they've understood them.** If they repeat back incomplete or inaccurate instructions, correct the error and ask them to repeat back again.

3. **Schedule an interim "check-in" meeting before the deadline** to provide feedback and give the staff an opportunity to improve the work before the actual deadline.

4. **Consider sharing with your staff a time where you had a similar challenge** and how you overcame it.

5. **Identify patterns of low quality and see if there are opportunities for staff training in those areas.** For example, if work is sloppy, has typos, or appears that it wasn't well thought through, attempt to address those issues specifically.

6. **Do not finish the task or make corrections for them.** Point out the errors and ask them to correct them. Be clear that it is their responsibility to turn in work assignments that are complete with high quality.

7. **Make sure your staff are taking in what you're telling them.** If you are giving feedback on work and you notice your staff member

is not taking notes, point it out to them and ask them to take notes, especially if remembering items has been a previous challenge.

8. **Work with staff to create a checklist of what you are looking for on assignments**. For example, you may want to ensure all memos are in the right format, with the correct date, and clearly state a point of contact for any questions. Review the checklist with staff who are having quality issues, and if that doesn't resolve it, ask them to complete the checklist and turn it in with the assignment.

9. **Consider asking employees with different strengths to "buddy" up to complete tasks.** Let them know that they should turn in the assignment only after both of them have signed off on it.

10. **This is an excellent opportunity to make this a learning experience** for your staff and to model appropriate behavior. Discuss difficult items forthrightly, be compassionate, listen, and move forward. Consider how to clarify your request, your approach, the importance of the work, and the need to get it done while balancing empathic and understanding of whatever is holding your staff back from being their best.

11. **Provide (de-identified, if needed) examples of high-quality work and low-quality work** and ask staff to identify how these are different. Help them understand that high-quality work is required.

12. **Ask your staff to make a list of everything on their plate so that you can understand how they are prioritizing this work.**

13. **Ask your staff to do a time chart** to identify how they are spending their time at work, rounded to nearest 30 minutes or so. That will give you an idea of which projects are taking the right amount of time, too little (which means quality may suffer), or too much (which means the staff don't understand the assignment or may be inefficient).

14. **Identify if there are underlying issues** that are leading to incomplete or low-quality work, such as being short staffed, overworked, or unclear on the expectations.

15. **You may need to provide written feedback and clarification of expectations** as part of a formal performance improvement plan for the employee. If your organization has a Human Resources office, they may be able to provide assistance on how to provide and document this feedback.

See also: **Challenge 29: How to help staff stay motivated**

Challenge 32: Being a good mentor

Challenge 47: Need to give difficult feedback to staff

Challenge 68: Create a strong culture

Take action: Assess the quality of your staff's work and identify how it could be increased. If you are doing more than a quick review of documents or products to confirm quality (such as rewriting, reorganizing, or correcting typos), your staff probably need to increase the quality of their work.

Challenge 37.
Staff frequently late

If you work in a company where timeliness is important—such as a call center, a retail establishment, or a restaurant—late staff throw a wrench in the works! For other companies, this is simply unprofessional behavior. Lateness is very common, unfortunately. Fortunately, there is a lot you can do to address it!

1. **Consider the implications of staff lateness.** Employees who arrive late may be stealing time from the company. Late employees may fall behind in their work, rush through work, or leave work unfinished. Lateness may cause resentment among other employees who have to cover for the late employee. Finally, the overall effectiveness of the team may be compromised if it becomes clear that there is a double standard for timeliness.

2. **Document expectations** including details of working hours, consequences of arriving late frequently, procedures for reporting anticipated lateness, how work time will be tracked, and potential disciplinary action for chronic lateness. Ensure staff have read the policies.

3. **Consider how much of a problem the lateness is.** For example, if the organizational culture is flexible in that staff can make up time by taking a shorter lunch or staying later, it may not be worth addressing as a performance issue but rather as an opportunity to clarify flexible working hours.

4. **Clarify what it means to be on time:** in the building? Clocked in? Physically at their work area even if they're still unpacking? At their work area and ready to start working? This is especially important for staff with time-sensitive duties like phone coverage.

5. **Schedule periodic "check-in" meetings with staff** regarding timeliness and discuss what is working and what is not working to ensure staff are on time. Reinforce accountability and learning.

6. **Document employee lateness and impact** in case you need this to provide counseling, performance feedback, or a written warning.

7. **This is an excellent opportunity to make this a learning experience for your staff and to model appropriate behavior.** Discuss difficult items forthrightly, be compassionate, listen, and move forward.

8. **If there is a clear expectation that employees are on time, make a point to "make the rounds" and say hello or good morning to everyone.** Once this becomes a habit, you might not need to say anything, as employees will know you know they were late and often will self-correct.

9. **Speak with the staff about your concerns,** showing them your documentation and referring to the organization's policy. Explain that you want to understand what is causing their lateness and find out if there's a way you could help them. Try to understand whether they have any personal problems, family issues, medical issues, or any other issues that might be causing their tardiness. Consider any potential ways the organization generally or you as leader/manager may be able to assist, such as emergency childcare, flex time, or work from home, even if only temporarily. Finally, together with the employee, create an action plan to prevent lateness from continuing.

10. **You may need to provide written feedback and clarification of expectations as part of a formal performance improvement plan for the employee.** If your organization has a Human Resources office, they may be able to provide assistance on how to provide and document this feedback.

See also: **Challenge 14: Start seeing yourself as a manager/ leader**

Challenge 29: How to help staff stay motivated

Challenge 47: Need to give difficult feedback to staff

Take action: If timeliness is important in your job, NOW is the time to address your staff's lateness.

Challenge 38.
Low staff morale

If everyone in your office is down in the dumps, work can be depressing. Whether it's a poor economy, unpopular company decisions, or a recent failure, low morale really stinks. Here are some ways to help lift your staff's spirits.

1. **Identify the issues that are causing low staff morale,** such as overwork, underpay, challenging conditions, harassment, lack of advancement opportunities, lack of clarity, poor leadership or one or more jerks on the team (it happens!).

2. **Spend time getting to know your staff.** It's important that they know you know who they are, that you are looking out for them, and that you care about them. It's a balance to do this while keeping personal and business separate, but you can do it!

3. **Talk with staff about the work environment** and be transparent regarding your concerns about morale. Ask opinion leaders about their perspective on morale and ask for suggestions on what might work.

4. **Schedule periodic "check-in" meetings to ask the staff for feedback about what is working and what is not working.** Provide feedback to them on your observations. Reinforce accountability and learning.

5. **Consider how to increase meaning and motivation for your staff.** Setting goals, reminding staff of the importance of their work, or bringing in beneficiaries of their work might be useful to increase their sense of meaning.

6. **Consider sharing the larger strategy with staff rather than only the day-to-day activities.** A broader perspective can help lift morale.

7. **Recognize your staff's work, effort, persistence, and achievements.** From a simple "Thank you" to bringing doughnuts or pizza (or a healthier alternative) for the office, recognition and gratitude can go a long way. Being mindful of employees' dietary restrictions is a very nice way to demonstrate your thoughtfulness.

8. **Train your managers and any staff leads on healthy and productive ways to give feedback and recognition to improve morale.**

9. **Help employees identify something to look forward to,** whether vacation, year-end bonus, summer picnic, promotion, or paid professional development.

10. **Deal with negative staff and energy drainers so they don't continue to bring others down.** Do this by talking with them individually about managing their attitude, or if that doesn't work, see if it's possible to isolate the others from the negativity (such as giving the energy drainer a pass from attending a meeting). Similarly, staff who have unaddressed performance problems can sap staff morale by making them feel like their work is not important. Address quickly and efficiently!

See also: **Challenge 12: Learn how to have difficult conversations**

Challenge 29: How to help staff stay motivated

Challenge 68: Create a strong culture

> **Take action: How will you know when morale is low? Are you asking your staff how they're doing? If not, start asking!**

Challenge 39.
Staff don't take initiative

Sometimes staff won't take initiative on projects. This could be due to a number of reasons including personal preference, previous experiences (perhaps with your predecessor), or passive aggressiveness. Here are some tips on how to help them take more initiative!

1. **State your expectations clearly at the beginning of the project,** including that you expect them to take initiative in certain circumstances and outline examples, how they should demonstrate initiative, and how they should keep you informed.

2. **Consider letting your staff know what you are looking for and asking them to come up with a plan to get it done.** Have them share their plan with you to approve first before they start working to help them get more comfortable with taking initiative. Over time and with practice, you can let them know what you want and trust they will follow through.

3. **Review your staff's job descriptions and ensure they are employed at the right level of seniority;** also, ensure that their job description includes taking initiative. If it doesn't, work with the Human Resources Department (if you have one) or with your supervisor to update job descriptions.

4. **Consider sharing with your staff a time where you had a similar challenge and how you addressed it.**

5. **Praise staff who take initiative in front of colleagues and clarify that you'd like to see that from all staff.**

6. **Praise staff in their performance reviews for making strides in initiative-taking.**

7. **This is an excellent opportunity to make this a learning experience for your staff** and to model appropriate behavior. Discuss difficult items forthrightly, be compassionate, listen, and move forward.

8. **Create specific opportunities in which your staff can take initiative.**

9. **Review with staff recent events** to discuss where they took initiative, how they did it, and what challenges they might have faced. Sometimes bosses may say they want initiative but then inadvertently discourage it or respond poorly when it happens. Ensure you're responding positively.

10. **If you have trouble communicating with staff about initiative,** ask your staff to come to you with a specific phrase, such as "I want to take initiative on xxx," so you can discuss how to proceed together.

11. **Schedule periodic "check-in" meetings with staff** to address what is working and what is not working about their taking initiative. Reinforce accountability and learning.

12. **You may need to provide written feedback and clarification of expectations about taking initiative as part of a formal performance improvement plan for the employee.** If your organization has a Human Resources office, they may be able to provide assistance.

See also: **Challenge 13: Set professional goals**

                             Challenge 25: Commit to continuous self-improvement

                             Challenge 32: Being a good mentor

Take action: What does initiative mean to you? Are you demonstrating it with your staff? What will it take for them to want to take initiative?

Challenge 40.
Staff make excuses for not completing work

Every now and then, work doesn't get completed. People who make excuses for not completing work are generally trying to avoid taking responsibility. For chronic excuse-makers, here are some strategies to help them be more effective (and make fewer excuses!).

1. **Review the assignment in detail with staff including deadlines and what quality completion of the assignment looks like.** Ask them what challenges they anticipate they will face.

2. **Ask staff to let you know when problems arise so they can be addressed.** Pay attention to how you respond to staff when they are bringing up problems to ensure you are encouraging them appropriately.

3. **Confirm to staff that they must let you know when anything comes up to delay completion of an assignment.** Be supportive when they bring a delay to you and help them solve to move past the delay.

4. **After you've provided the expectations, ask your staff questions to ensure they've understood the assignment and what to do if a challenge arises.** For example, you can ask, "So if Finance has not provided the numbers you need tomorrow, what would you do then?" Review likely scenarios with them to ensure they understand how to proceed.

5. **Ask your staff to make a list of everything on their plate so that you can understand where they are prioritizing this work.**

6. **Try to understand if there are additional issues behind staff's making excuses,** such as feeling overworked, under-resourced, not

clear on the assignment, or previous experiences of overly critical supervisors.

7. **Consider asking an employee** who is effective in completing work to do a staff teach-in on successful strategies.

8. **This is an excellent opportunity to make this a learning experience** for your staff and to model appropriate behavior. Discuss difficult items forthrightly, be compassionate, listen, and move forward.

9. **Have periodic check-ins prior to completing the project.** Share with your staff what you expect them to bring to the check-ins: an agenda with each aspect of the assignment, status, and challenges outlined. That will help you have more efficient meetings.

10. **You may need to provide written feedback and clarification of expectations for completing work as part of a formal performance improvement plan for the employee.** If your organization has a Human Resources office, they may be able to provide assistance.

See also: **Challenge 13: Set professional goals**

Challenge 22: Learn how to say no

Challenge 43: Staff don't work as a team

Take action: Is it possible there's something behind the excuses? If the work allows it, play detective and figure out what's going on.

Challenge 41.
Sexual harassment

It can happen to anyone across all spectrums of gender and sexuality: a colleague doesn't acknowledge that no means no or continues to make sexual comments around you or even touches you without your permission. This is one of the most frightening and upsetting experiences people have at work. Many of us struggle with wanting the perpetrator to stop and the very real possibility that speaking up can hurt *your* career. Here are some ways to address this stressful situation, whether you or someone on your team is the victim.

1. **It's important to speak up when you hear inappropriate comments.** If you don't speak up, it often gives the impression that you are condoning them even if you are not.

2. **Consider the difference between a request and a demand.** You can start with a request ("Please don't use that word") and then escalate to a demand if needed. For example, "We all enjoy joking around, but jokes about racial groups are not funny, and I won't listen anymore." Then walk away. Another example, "Please don't use that word around me. It makes me uncomfortable." If the person claims they are kidding around, you can say, "I don't appreciate jokes about [x]. Please stop." Then walk away.

3. **Generally the process if you are dealing with sexual harassment is** to (a) ask the harasser to stop if it is safe to do so, then (b) report the behavior to the appropriate office (Equal Employment Opportunity Office, Office of Diversity and Inclusion) and/or your supervisor with a specific request. If there is no official response or if the response is weak (asking you to stop creating trouble, not taking it seriously),

you may want to consider obtaining a lawyer and/or leaving the organization.

4. **Document what happened** including the date, location, people present, and what happened, even if in your own file. Have "receipts" you can go back to.

5. **Get support from others,** including friends or family. Be cautious discussing the situation too broadly within the organization, especially if it could possibly lead to legal action for discrimination. If you happen to know a friend who experienced sexual harassment, you may want to let them know what is happening to you and ask what they recommend.

6. **Know your rights on behalf of yourself and your staff:** In the U.S., repeated unwanted sexual comments, propositions, or touching can be considered sexual harassment and can be against the law. Some behavior is egregious even if committed only once. Know what is and is not acceptable behavior legally. The U.S. Equal Employment Opportunity Commission has definitions.

7. **Check your organization's policies for how they address sexual harassment.** This policy will outline acceptable and unacceptable behavior and indicate whom to contact if there is a problem.

8. **Observe the culture of your organization to identify how much sexualized talk (including jokes and memes) is commonplace and accepted.** The more it is accepted, the more difficult it might be for you to succeed in getting the perpetrator to stop. If this is the case, consider changing organizations.

9. **If you are in the U.S. or employed by a U.S.-based company,** you have the right to contact the Equal Employment Opportunity Commission if you feel you are being

discriminated against because of your gender, including repeated, unwanted sexual comments or propositions.

10. **Be very clear with messages you are sending to individuals regarding your personal life.** If there is ever a misunderstanding about your intentions or your boundaries, state explicitly that you want their behavior to stop. If it continues, escalate to someone else at your organization.

11. **Strength in numbers**: Spend time with people in a similar group as you, such as age, professional level, etc., so you're not alone with this person.

12. **Consider whether it might make sense to transfer units** within the organization if other methods don't work to get the person to stop.

13. **Consider national organizations and support groups that can provide information and resources**, such as #metoo (metoomvmt.org); the Rape, Abuse & Incest National Network (rainn.org), leanin.org, and others.

See also: **Challenge 11: Clarify your values**

Challenge 18: Build allies and friendships at work

Challenge 24: Manage and overcome overwhelm

Challenge 62: Boss bullies or undermines you

Challenge 68: Create a strong culture

Take action: Get support from a close friend or colleague so you can decide what to do.

Challenge 42.
Staff are aggressive, racist, sexist, homophobic, or hostile

I hope you never have to deal with aggressive, racist, sexist, homophobic, or hostile staff. If you do, I want you to have tools to deal with the situation in the moment and to take appropriate action, so it stops.

1. **It's important to speak up when you hear inappropriate comments.** If you don't speak up, it often gives the impression that you are condoning them even if you are not. This is especially important as a leader or manager.

2. **Always document what happened** including the date, location, people present, and what happened.

3. **It won't feel necessary, but state clearly what you are requesting.** For example, if you are talking to a peer, you could say, "Please don't use that word at work. It makes me uncomfortable." If you are talking to your staff, say more directly, "Do not use that word at work again. It is inappropriate and unacceptable."

4. **If the person claims they are kidding around,** you can say, "I don't appreciate jokes about [x]. Please stop."

5. **If there are staff around who are immediately affected by the offensive comment or action, state your piece in front of others intentionally to clarify the behavior that is not acceptable.** If necessary, discuss the issue with the staff member privately, and document the conversation.

6. **In some circumstances, it may be helpful to consider the difference between a request and a demand.** You can start

with a request ("Please don't use that word") and then escalate to a demand if needed. For example, "We all enjoy joking around, but jokes about racial groups are not funny, and it's not allowed at work." Then walk away.

7. **Get support from others, including friends or family.** Be cautious discussing the situation too broadly within the organization, especially if it could possibly lead to legal action for discrimination.

8. **Negotiation and conflict management expert Catherine Morrison provided an example of how to respond to insults disguised as "jokes" that's helpful in many circumstances.** Simply connect an observation with a statement of its impact: "I see you smiling, but that feels like a dig."

9. **If staff are being loud and obnoxious—but not offensive— you can rein in the conversation.** For example, "Let's get back to the agenda. Next was . . . "

10. **Consider contacting your boss, Human Resources (which is there to protect the organization), or a lawyer (who is there to protect you)** for assistance in managing persistent discriminatory language or actions. If you need to find a lawyer, contact a local university law school for an inexpensive or low-cost referral or Google "best employment lawyer" with the name of your town and call to ask for a free consultation.

See also: **Challenge 7: Developing/determining your managing/leadership style**

Challenge 11: Clarify your values

Challenge 68: Create a strong culture

Take action: There's no excuse for aggressive, racist, sexist, homophobic, or other hostile behavior. Nip it in the bud and get it out of your workplace. Your staff will thank you.

Challenge 43.
Staff don't work as a team

Most leaders are challenged at some point in their career to develop teams out of workers who might not know or even like each other. There are great resources on team building (see the For further reading section). Here are some tips to get you started!

1. **Help your team understand the story of who they have been, and help them identify and develop a new story.** For example, their current story could be, "We are always the underperformers in the company," and their new story can become, "We come together to excel."

2. **Read *The Five Dysfunctions of a Team: A Leadership Fable* by Patrick Lencioni** for ideas on how teams can work together (and what to do when they don't).

3. **For disagreements between individuals, talk with each of them separately and encourage them to manage the disagreement together.** Advise them to go out for coffee and work out their differences. (Of course, if one person is being hostile or threatening, this is not a good approach—that would require further intervention to ensure the employees are protected).

4. **Consider sharing with your staff a time where you had a similar challenge with coworkers**, a seemingly unachievable goal, or whatever is challenging your team.

5. **Praise staff when you see them including others.** For example, you can say, "Thanks so much for making sure everyone was invited to the party" or "Thanks for really pulling together on this project!"

6. **This is an excellent opportunity to make this a learning experience for your staff and to model appropriate behavior.** Discuss difficult items forthrightly, be compassionate, listen, and move forward.

7. **Remember that part of developing a strong team is retaining and developing strong staff.** Your best staff are lifelong learners who will need challenges, and it's up to you as manager to provide them with these challenges.

8. **Building a team and providing feedback go hand in hand.** Provide feedback frequently so employees have no question of where they stand with you regarding their performance. You may need to provide written feedback and clarification of expectations as part of a formal performance review for the employee. Having provided feedback frequently will make this an easier process. It will also help the staff trust you because you are direct with them.

9. **Always be kind.** Keep your own emotions and pressures in check so you don't let them bleed onto your employees.

10. **Ask for feedback from your team on what is going well, what's not going well, and how they think work can go better.** Note: before you do this, make sure you're willing to change. This can be individual conversations and occasional group discussions. Encourage the team to discuss what is getting in their way and how it can be improved, without going into personal attacks on individuals. This will help them learn to problem solve as a team as well!

See also: **Challenge 3: Skills needed to be a good manager and leader**

                        Challenge 22: Learn how to say no

                        Challenge 24: Manage and overcome overwhelm

Take action: It's not personal—it's work! What's one thing you can do to help your staff get on the same page?

Challenge 44.
Constant complaining

We all know someone who is constantly complaining about the job, the weather, the commute, the world ... I've known staff who complained about a problematic task at work, complained about efforts to resolve the problems, and complained about the solution without missing a beat. What do you do when you have a complainer (or more) on your staff?

1. **Demonstrate empathy.** This may be the furthest thing from your mind with a complainer, but sometimes the only thing more miserable than being *around* a complainer is *being* the complainer. It must feel awful to see only what's not working. Approach the situation with compassion.

2. **Continue to demonstrate genuine positivity.** Complainers may be suspicious of you at first, but persevere until they trust that you really, truly, can be positive.

3. **Look for people doing well—try to "catch them doing good"** and make a positive comment, the more specific, the better (but not about personal characteristics or appearance).

4. **Humor can help reset complaining.** Using positive humor—no put-downs of anyone—can be as simple as starting a meeting by saying, "Does anyone have a good clean joke?"

5. **Invite the complainer to be a part of improving something they've complained about.** Keep up positive comments with your faith that they can resolve the issue and make things better. When a complainer was able to successfully resolve a problem, I brought it up over and over and over again in meetings: "Remember when Tim fixed the budget glitch? That was amazing!" which makes

it harder for the complainer to keep complaining. (When I said this, Tim sometimes even cracked a smile!) Asking complainers to be part of the solution may also inadvertently reduce their complaining.

6. **Praise staff who demonstrate patience and who do not complain.** For example, you can say, "I know this is a tough time, and I appreciate your positive attitude and patience as we work through it."

7. **This is an excellent opportunity to make this a learning experience** for your staff and to model appropriate behavior. Discuss difficult items forthrightly, be compassionate, listen, and move forward.

8. **After a big project or accomplishment, have a review with the staff to discuss what went well and not well** with an aim of how to do things better next time. That gives the complainer an appropriate context in which to complain and can help find a good outlet for making complaints useful. Make sure to balance the meeting with what went well and how to apply what was learned.

9. **Schedule periodic "check-in" meetings to hear staff perspective and provide feedback about how things are going and what can be better.** Reinforce accountability and learning.

10. **If the complaining is extremely negative, nasty, offensive, or chronic, you will need to discuss the issue with the employee.** Provide written feedback and clarification of expectations (including attitude) and the impact of their chronic complaining on others as part of an informal or formal performance improvement plan for the employee. If your organization has a Human Resources office, they may be able to provide assistance.

11. **Don't complain about the complainer (or with them).** Learn deflections, such as, "It sounds like you should talk to Sam about your concern" or "I'm sorry to hear that" or "Sounds like some things aren't going well. What is going well?"

See also: **Challenge 11: Clarify your values**

                      Challenge 20: How to run a good meeting

                      Challenge 24: Manage and overcome overwhelm

Take action: Check yourself for complaining before you start working to help others reduce their complaining. Sometimes we aren't aware of our own actions!

Challenge 45.
Shift work/shared staff/remote team

It's a special challenge to manage and lead staff who work different shifts, who are shared across multiple supervisors, or who live across the country! With increasing telework and novel organizational structures, these situations are becoming more common. Hone your skills here, and managing a team in person will be a piece of cake!

1. **Understand the importance of creating a positive culture,** especially for those on shift work, who have multiple supervisors, or who work remotely. A positive culture keeps employees engaged, motivated, and performing at a high level.

2. **Have a virtual break room,** such as an online Slack or Skype chat or online bulletin board where all staff can post about anything and respond to each other. One center where I worked had a caption contest weekly, which engaged people to both submit captions and vote on their favorites—I quickly learned who the clever wordsmiths were!

3. **Consider a team challenge,** such as counting daily steps on a pedometer, training for a 5k race, or collecting pennies for a charity. These kinds of challenges can give staff something light to discuss and can help the team feel closer with each other.

4. **Transparency helps.** Posting task information and work schedules on a shared online resource can give all staff the opportunity to see what's happening and ask questions, thus reducing tension because of others' availability. It can also increase predictability and allow people to get in touch with each other on a regular basis.

5. **Clarify performance expectations for everyone and check in on staff periodically to confirm they are completing their work**

with sufficient quality and in a timely manner. Clarify if you are measuring their performance on time (e.g., hours worked) or on performance (e.g., accomplishments).

6. **When staff report to multiple individuals, keep communication among supervisors open and transparent.** Ensure the staff knows the supervisors are connecting frequently and are available to address any unclear priorities between them. This will also help reduce staff playing one boss against the other.

7. **If possible, have everyone meet in person or at least in a few shifts once a year,** or have an online call where everyone can see each other's faces and get to know each other better. You can also set up pairs who work in complementary areas to "interview" each other and ask each other questions about their work and how to improve performance.

8. **Focus on your staff's strengths.** Make a point to comment on what you appreciate about your staff, how well your team communicates, or whatever else is going well. Provide specific positive feedback to help keep staff motivated and know that you see them.

9. **Support and mentor your staff.** Make sure they are getting something from work that they want, whether they're in it for the satisfaction, professional advancement, or only the salary.

10. **Keep communicating.** Let staff know you're there for them, can help them, and support their growth.

See also: **Challenge 15: Starting a new job as manager or leader**

Challenge 24: Manage and overcome overwhelm

Challenge 43: Staff don't work as a team

Take action: Have you ever worked remotely? What were the personal challenges you faced, and how did you alleviate them? Or, ask a friend who works remotely for advice on how their team has overcome remote challenges.

Challenge 46.
Staff play one boss against another

If you have staff who also report to other people, that opens the door for the employee to play bosses against each other. This is one of the easier challenges to solve, because it's all about communication.

1. **Know what it looks like to play one boss against the other.** For many it can start feeling like working with a child: you say yes, only to find the other boss said no already. Some staff speak negatively about each boss to the other, try to start conflict between the two bosses, or shirk on work for one boss, saying they are working for the other—and telling the other boss the same thing.

2. **Talk with the person's other boss about your and their expectations for the individual.** Ideally, the two of you can meet with the staff and clarify together that you're on the same page with your expectations.

3. **Clarify the primary boss.** Typically, this is the person who oversees paid time off, benefits, performance reviews, and other administrative functions. Ensure you include all bosses in decisions to the extent they want to be involved.

4. **Keep communication open.** Identify how best to copy the other boss on emails and ask the staff member to copy you both on emails so everything is transparent.

5. **Consider having a shared place for communication** (such as a Slack or Skype channel) for the employee and their bosses to ensure everyone can look up a history of communication any time.

6. **Share task information and work schedules online or by email to ensure everyone can see what's happening and ask questions.**

It can also increase predictability and allow people to get in touch with each other on a regular basis.

7. **Check in on staff and their other bosses periodically** to confirm things are going smoothly and to address any concerns. If phone calls and emails don't work, have an in-person or online meeting where everyone is present.

8. **This is an excellent opportunity to make this a learning experience for your staff and to model appropriate behavior.** Discuss difficult items forthrightly, be compassionate, listen, and move forward.

9. **If you and the other boss(es) have differing opinions on how something should proceed,** consider whether it's appropriate to divide task strategies by boss or to use the difference of opinion as an opportunity for the staff to learn different approaches.

10. **If the staff is persistent in being manipulative with multiple bosses, you and their other bosses may need to discuss the issue directly with the employee.** Provide written feedback and clarification of expectations (including attitude) and the impact of their actions on others as part of an informal or formal performance improvement plan for the employee. If your organization has a Human Resources office, they may be able to provide assistance.

See also: **Challenge 14: Start seeing yourself as a manager/ leader**

Challenge 25: Commit to continuous self-improvement

Challenge 43: Staff don't work as a team

Take action: Find out which staff may have multiple bosses. Consider talking with these bosses to see if anyone else is having a similar challenge. Maybe you could address it together?

Challenge 47.
Need to give difficult feedback to staff

Many people dislike giving performance reviews and difficult feedback to staff. And yet, it's one of the critical responsibilities of a manager.

1. **Read classic books** *Difficult Conversations: How to Discuss What Matters Most by* Douglas Stone, Bruce Patton & Sheila Ileen and *Crucial Conversations: Tools for Talking When Stakes Are High* by Al Switzler, Joseph Grenny, and Ron McMillan (listed in the For further reading section).

2. **Prepare your talking points before the conversation** and make sure you are only giving feedback that is accurate, fair, and actionable.

3. **This is an excellent opportunity to make this a learning experience for your staff and to model appropriate behavior.** Discuss difficult items forthrightly, be compassionate, listen, and move forward.

4. **Consider whether the Human Resources office has online training or can provide consultation to assist you with providing feedback.**

5. **Identify someone who seems good at providing feedback and ask them how they do it.**

6. **Notice how you respond to feedback from others**. If you are not receiving feedback, ask someone for it. For example, you can say to a trusted colleague, "I'm working on running more effective meetings. How do you think that one went? Do you have any suggestions for how I can make it better?"

7. **Role-play the situation with someone outside work with you being the feedback recipient.** Stop the conversation as needed to brainstorm how you might address different ways in which the feedback recipient might respond.

8. **If the staff member has a history of shouting or physical outbursts,** discuss the situation ahead of time with Human Resources and consider if you would like to have security in the area in case the person becomes upset or violent.

9. **Identify ahead of time what you think the best-case scenario is for the difficult feedback.** Sometimes, it might not be possible both to give honest feedback and to not hurt their feelings. Identify what you want to occur as a result of your conversation and identify how to get there.

10. **Be kind.** We all have our struggles and you may not know what is happening in someone's personal life.

11. **It may be appropriate to ask if something else is going on with the person.** If the person states or suggests there may be a personal problem outside of work that is affecting their performance, suggest they can talk with the Employee Assistance Program or Human Resources. Indicate they do not need or have to share details with you (sometimes people want to share all the details to manipulate you into feeling sorry for them so they can continue to deflect responsibility). Express concern and work with them to address the task at hand.

12. **In difficult conversations, make sure to ask staff what questions they have.** Encourage them to contact you with any questions in the future.

See also: **Challenge 12: Learn how to have difficult
conversations**

Challenge 11: Clarify your values

Challenge 26: Hiring strong staff

**Take action: What are you worried about when giving
feedback? That you'll be too harsh? Too easy? Ask a
colleague for advice about how they manage giving difficult
feedback.**

Challenge 48.
Coaching staff to move on when it's time

I view the role of a manager and leader as twofold: First, of course, is completing the mission, the work, or the job. Second, is to develop staff and help them learn and grow. Staff who have excelled may reach a plateau and need to move on to continue their own growth. For other staff, it might become clear that this position is not a good fit for them. Tough conversations? You bet.

1. **Speak with your boss and possibly Human Resources (if your company has HR) or your organization's legal office.** Coaching staff to move on is a serious move, and you'll want to know that your organization has your back. There may be other issues to consider and other steps to take before helping them move on. There may also be things you can't say, such as suggesting it's time for retirement, because that could be considered a violation of the employee's rights.

2. **Consider whether it's really time for the person to move on.** Is their work not up to par? Are they burned out or unmotivated? Do they need more challenges? Other solutions may be available to remedy these situations and retain the staff member in their current position.

3. **Consider the "red button" test.** If you could press a red button and the person would disappear from your team—and be happy and healthy but *somewhere else*—would you do it? If so, consider it might be time for them to move on.

4. **Say to staff, "I want you to be happy and successful. Hopefully you can be happy and successful here. If not, I will help you be happy and successful somewhere else."** Sometimes that's enough for someone to confess they're not happy or that the job isn't a

good fit. They can take you up on your offer to help them with their next steps. Remember you're responsible for opening doors and *helping* them, not doing it *for* them.

5. **Successful staff might be open to hearing about other opportunities** to take on more challenging work in their current position, which could open the door to a conversation about them moving into a different position. Tell them what you see as their strengths, identify opportunities for them to move ahead, and ask them about their goals. Accept if it's not a good time for them to take on a different job or new responsibilities and continue to provide support and opportunity.

6. **For low performers, you can clarify the performance concerns and provide some options**: (a) they could resign now or in a few days after thinking it over, (b) they could look for another position with you mutually agreeing on a deadline for them to do this, or (c) if they don't like either of those options, you will have to begin a performance improvement plan or disciplinary process immediately.

7. **This is an excellent opportunity to make this a learning experience** for your staff and to model appropriate behavior. Discuss difficult items forthrightly, be compassionate, listen, and move forward.

8. **Consider sharing with your staff a time where you had a similar challenge**, such as when you realized a position wasn't a good fit, or when it was time to move on to something more challenging. Describing your experience might help them realize it's not their personal failing, but rather your interest in helping them be successful.

9. **There are legal limits in what you can say related to a person's fit for the position** or a suggestion they might need to move on to minimize discrimination. Be sensitive to how your conversations can sound to the other person, especially someone who is older (age discrimination laws apply to individuals over 40) or who is a

minority on the team (e.g., the only woman or only person of color). Be especially careful that you are discussing their performance, not their personal characteristics, as associated with your ideas of them benefiting from moving on to a different position.

10. **You may want to consider obtaining a coach** who can help you through this challenge—it's a really difficult conversation. You'll also want to practice what you'll say with a trusted colleague or friend outside of work.

See also: **Challenge 12: Learn how to have difficult conversations**

Challenge 47: Need to give difficult feedback to staff

Challenge 49: Firing staff

Take action: Do you have any staff who are ready to move on? Who fail the "red button" test? If so, identify what you will do about it.

Challenge 49.
Firing staff

One of the most difficult tasks as a manager can be firing staff. Whether they are being laid off or fired for cause, the process is stressful either way. Here are some suggestions to proceed in a kind and professional manner.

1. **Communicate clearly to all staff about your expectations before you ever get to the place where staff performance is an issue.** Also make sure you understand—and that your staff understand—your organization's policies for addressing performance issues and procedures for firing or laying off staff.

2. **Consider whether it's really time for the person to move on.** Is their work not up to par? Are they burned out or unmotivated? Do they need more challenges? Many of these situations can have other solutions.

3. **Consider whether individuals should be offered the opportunity to improve.** Many workplaces require a combination of verbal warnings, written warnings, and a performance improvement plan to provide plenty of opportunities to improve prior to letting someone go unless there are egregious circumstances, such as theft, assault, or harassment. Firing staff for performance should rarely come as a surprise to them.

4. **Talk with your boss, the Human Resources department if you have one, and possibly the legal department about how to proceed with letting staff go.** There may be other issues to consider and other steps to take before helping them move on. Policies and procedures can help, but nothing takes the place of walking through a conversation with someone, especially if you haven't done it before.

5. **Practice what you will say, and if possible, role-play how you think the other person might respond.** Make sure you can hold up your end of the conversation with minimal emotional displays (crying, anger), and that you can stay professional throughout, even if it's a difficult conversation.

6. **People who are fired or laid off are often eligible for certain benefits,** such as unemployment insurance, severance, COBRA (health insurance), outplacement services, or retirement investment notices. If you have a Human Resources department, they should be able to provide you with benefits employees are entitled to and information the organization is required to provide to departing employees. If you don't have a Human Resources department, ask your supervisor. Knowing this information going into the conversation with your employee will be helpful because they will likely ask about it, and providing this info will help temper the emotional difficulty of just learning they've been fired.

7. **Layoffs and firing are opportunities to model appropriate and respectful behavior.** Discuss difficult items forthrightly as much as possible, be compassionate, listen, and move forward.

8. **Consider how you will manage this situation with your other staff.** This may vary depending on the circumstances of the firing and the size/composition/culture of your team. You may want to make an announcement in a group, or it may be more appropriate to let colleagues know individually. It's important to give staff time to grieve, whether it's about the departure of a well-liked employee, relief that a challenging colleague is gone, or concerns they might be fired next. This would be a good time to remind staff that you understand everyone has feelings, and it's important to be respectful in any discussion at the workplace and limit gossip.

9. **Do not indicate what happened with the fired employee or why**—"Terry is no longer with the company" will suffice. Remind staff that their jobs are not in jeopardy, and that decisions to let someone go happen only after much thought and attempts to

work things out. I find that reminding them that people don't get fired out of nowhere both calms anxiety and is a subtle way of telling them that Terry had many chances to address and improve his behavior (despite what version of the story he may have told them).

10. **Ensure there is clear communication regarding how the departing employee's tasks will be managed, on hold, or distributed,** and whether there will be another individual hired to fill the position or whether the position is being eliminated.

11. **Survivor's guilt is real.** People who remain employed after a layoff or firing may feel guilty, anxious, or upset that they are still there while others have been let go. They may feel uncomfortable at work because they lost their coworkers, and may feel angry with the management they view as responsible for the situation. Be compassionate.

12. **Take time and space outside of work and not in front of your staff to do your own processing of the situation.** You can consider how you handled it and what you could have done better, relief it's over, regret over what happened, sadness, or anything else you are feeling with a colleague, friend or other person who is not your staff.

See also: **Challenge 12: Learn how to have difficult conversations**

Challenge 47: Need to give difficult feedback to staff

Challenge 48: Coaching staff to move on when it's time

Take action: Talk to someone not on your team who has been fired. What was productive, helpful, and kind that happened? What was most difficult for them? See what you can learn.

Part V.
Colleague challenges

Challenge 50.
Colleague doesn't contribute

From grade-school projects to day-to-day work, sometimes our colleagues don't pull their own weight. No need to get angry—just try some strategies to help things move forward.

1. **Start by assuming the person has something else getting in the way of completing their work as opposed to refusing to work.** Check with them and see if there is something else going on.

2. **Ask the colleague if they are having trouble completing their part of the work and why.** There might be a way to assist them, suggest resources, or otherwise address the impasse.

3. **Clarify with the colleague who is responsible for what and make notes.** If there are differences of opinion, try to work it out with your colleague.

4. **If your colleague still doesn't do their part, follow up with an email** saying, "As we discussed, you said you could finish [x] by today and it hasn't been completed. I haven't had the opportunity to review it. Could you please send it to me so I can review?" If possible, tie the request to a key result or deliverable that is dependent on their task being delivered: "It's important we finish this project on time so we can proceed to the next step." Be extra careful about tone in emails and ask someone to read it over before you send it to be safe.

5. **Go to your boss for assistance in sorting out the situation.**

6. **Consider forwarding resources to assist with a project** or suggesting someone to contact if they are having difficulty.

7. If appropriate (such as if you are getting stonewalled), ask a status question in a more public setting so that your roles can be agreed upon in public. You can say, "John was working on this part of the project. John, could you give us an update on the status of the project?"

8. Set clear boundaries and be sure not to take on the other person's work responsibilities. Being professional and thoughtful doesn't mean you do their work. Find that balance.

9. Move your conversations from less formal to more formal by having a meeting with the colleague, providing an agenda, and sharing notes on what was agreed. If appropriate, copy your boss on the emails. Document everything!

10. Adjust your expectations about the kind of relationship you can have with this colleague. Take steps to ensure fairness, and also know you might not have the kind of collegial relationship you would like.

11. If this is a pattern with this particular colleague not doing their work, ask to be reassigned to a project not working with this colleague.

12. You may want to consider obtaining a coach who can help you through difficult colleague situations.

See also: **Challenge 11: Clarify your values**

Challenge 18: Build allies and friendships at work

Challenge 51: Colleagues take credit for your work

> **Take action: Given the situation you're currently in, what feels like the best strategy for both you and your colleague? Come up with your unique action plan.**

Challenge 51.
Colleagues take credit for your work

You worked with a colleague on a project, but they present it as their own and don't acknowledge your contributions. It is so frustrating when someone else takes credit for your work! There are several ways to address this issue, so it doesn't happen more than once.

1. For a new project, attempt to clarify who will do what parts of the projects, and how credit will be allocated.

2. Try to work with colleagues who share responsibility and credit, if possible.

3. Talk to the person who took credit for your work to let them know you saw what they did and that it wasn't cool.

4. Build relationships with colleagues; they may be less likely to take credit for your work if they have a genuine connection with you.

5. Keep notes about who is doing what for each project. This documentation may come in handy later to refresh your memory if you need it.

6. Limit how you share information you may find sensitive if you think they might not use it well or might use it against you.

7. Consider talking to your boss or the person running the project to clarify what happened and ask for advice regarding how to proceed.

8. Observe the environment where you work to identify if this is a common and accepted occurrence or whether it is generally

discouraged. If it is a common and accepted occurrence, consider whether this is the right work environment for you.

9. **Identify which types of projects can be done alone versus which need to be split amongst employees.** Think about which person has the proper expertise for the subject area, so roles and contribution can be defined early.

10. **Adjust your expectations about the kind of relationship you can have with this colleague.** Take steps to ensure fairness, and also know you might not have the kind of collegial relationship you would like.

11. **Consider meeting with colleagues to discuss how credit is allocated.** Can you all share credit, or take turns having primary credit across different projects so you all benefit? You can also develop this meeting into an informal peer mentoring group.

12. **If you frequently feel like people are taking advantage of you,** you may want to consider obtaining a therapist who can help you through this challenge so that you can break the patterns and feel better.

See also: **Challenge 11: Clarify your values**

Challenge 18: Build allies and friendships at work

Challenge 50: Colleague doesn't contribute

> **Take action: Write out your revenge–every last detail–and reflect: Is this how you want to be seen or heard? (Probably not.) Instead of revenge, what's the best way for you to express this issue? Get clear before taking action.**

Challenge 52.
Colleagues are extremely competitive

Organizations and fields vary in the degree of competition between employees. High levels of competition can feel very uncomfortable if you're not used to it.

1. **Observe the environment where you work to identify if this is a common and accepted occurrence or whether it is generally discouraged.** Consider if being more competitive is consistent with your values or your approach to work. If not, this may not be the job, field, or organization for you.

2. **You may want to increase your competitiveness.** Consider what is in line with your values and how to improve your skills at competing.

3. **Identify how merit raises, promotions, and praise are provided and delivered.** For example, some units or organizations manage merit raises as a zero-sum game (where one wins and the other loses), whereas other groups provide merit raises equally to all members of the team based on collective team performance. Consider if the way your field, organization, or unit manages these limited resources is in line with your values.

4. **Consider whether what you are observing is healthy tension,** in which two teams simply have opposing goals (e.g., one team needs to get it submitted fast and another team is responsible for checking all details for accuracy). Healthy tension should still be respectful. Bring both teams together to voice their concerns so that both groups can be more successful together.

5. **Identify a colleague who is competitive and ask them about their approach to work relationships.**

6. **Talk to someone you trust outside of work for an outside opinion.**

7. **Consider gender, race, ethnicity, sexual orientation, and disability status** regarding how you're perceiving the situation or how you are being perceived. Resources on building equity and understanding privilege are in the For further reading section.

8. **Consider the value in being a neutral player.** That could mean you are less likely to be promoted, or it could mean you become trusted by everyone. Identify if neutrality is a workable stance for you.

9. **Consider taking part in extracurricular sports activities with your organization,** such as on the softball team. It may give you a different perspective of how competition works in the organization.

10. **Adjust your expectations about the kind of relationship you can have with these colleagues.** Take steps to ensure fairness, but know you might not have the kind of collegial relationship you would like.

11. **You may want to consider obtaining a coach who can help you through how you can best respond to your colleagues' competitiveness.**

See also: **Challenge 11: Clarify your values**

                 Challenge 12: Learn how to have difficult conversations

                 Challenge 18: Build allies and friendships at work

Take action: What makes you feel the most confident? It could be anything! Write it all out below. Notice anything that's calling you in to connect even more to your confidence level?

Challenge 53.
Backstabbing

Unfortunately, some people are jerks. Others are generally nice people who sometimes do jerky things. A colleague told me how hurt he was when someone told him that they were supporting his promotion yet wrote a very negative letter recommending against promotion to the committee. Ouch! Backstabbing, which is when someone criticizes or undermines you while feigning friendship, can be painful. It's best not to let it happen more than once.

1. **Limit the information you share with colleagues to reduce the amount of ammunition they have on you.** Be extremely judicious with sharing any personal information, including about problems you are struggling with or any personal issues.

2. **Consider what the backstabber's motive might be**—is it personal to them, business, competition, or is this just how they are? Understanding their motives may help you understand how to counter them and protect yourself.

3. **Consider whether it would make sense to confront the backstabber.** If you do, stick to the facts and identify what you observed and ask for their perspective, such as by saying, "It seemed like this was intentional; can you help me understand what happened?" If they don't respond kindly and by attempting to make the situation better, stay away.

4. **Consider whether it is possible to avoid the backstabber** if possible and if doing so would not harm you professionally.

5. **Talk to someone you trust outside of work for an outside opinion.**

6. **Pull together copies of documents that demonstrate your role in this situation—have "receipts" you can go back to.**

7. **Consider meeting with colleagues to compare experiences.** You can also develop this meeting into an informal mentoring group.

8. **If it is possible and if the backstabbing is isolated to one or two people,** consider switching groups or teams in your organization so you are not working with the person.

9. **Consider talking with your boss about the organization's perspective on civility and courtesy generally to understand their perspective and see if they may be an ally.** Speak tactfully and be cautious not to fuel workplace drama with your boss.

10. **Adjust your expectations about the kind of relationship you can have with this colleague.** Take steps to ensure fairness and reduce their poor behavior, but know you might not have the kind of collegial relationship you would like.

11. **Consider whether it may make sense to limit your public expressions of disappointment or hurt.** Sometimes it is better to not give backstabbers the satisfaction.

12. **Observe the environment where you work to identify if this is a common and accepted occurrence or whether it is generally discouraged.** If it is a common and accepted occurrence, consider whether this is the right work environment for you.

See also: **Challenge 18: Build allies and friendships at work**

Challenge 62: Boss bullies or undermines you

Challenge 65: Boss has unreasonable expectations

Take action: Exercise allows you to release frustration and create a clear mind. What's your favorite form of movement? Go do that, then come back and write down your approach and dealing with that backstabber. Notice how your energy changed?

Challenge 54.
Over-disclosing colleagues

Sometimes you learn things about your colleagues you didn't want to know. They keep sharing information about their family, their medical problems, or their lives that is not work-appropriate or that is way too much.

1. **Do not reciprocate by sharing personal information when a colleague over-discloses.** Instead, provide neutral responses ("Oh, that sounds difficult") or responses that end the conversation ("I'm sorry, I have to go to a meeting").

2. **Observe what kind of information about personal lives is generally disclosed and how it happens.** For example, do bosses typically ask how their staff will use their vacation days or what illness they were experiencing when they call out sick? Both of those are indicators that this environment may tolerate over-disclosure (or at least that this boss does). Your comfort with high disclosure may vary; high disclosure could become a problem if you have private health or personal information you'd rather not be shared, or if personal information is used in work decisions (e.g., "We understand you're coming back from leave after your mother's passing, so we gave a high-profile project to someone else"). Identify if this is organization-wide or limited to this group only.

3. **Have a selection of vague answers ready that provide minimal information if you are asked these questions.** For example, if you are asked about what you did on vacation, you can say you stayed at home or traveled with friends if you don't want to discuss your personal living situation.

4. **If people respond to your minimal information with judgmental comments** (for example, if you tell them you went to the beach on vacation and they say, "Oh, that sounds expensive!" or "How did you afford that?") end the conversation and share even less next time.

5. **Do not share personal information in areas where you are not sure you are alone (e.g., in a bathroom).**

6. **Talk to someone you trust outside of work for an outside opinion of what is appropriate sharing at their workplace.**

7. **You may want to have a variety of responses that help redirect the colleague back to work conversations,** such as, "Okay. Now about this report . . ." or "Huh. As I was saying . . ."

8. **Be aware of and possibly limit the amount of personal information you share passively,** such as photos and mementos on your desk. This can help set the expectation that you are there to work.

9. **Unfriend or unfollow a colleague on social media if you feel you're being exposed to too much personal information.**

10. **If someone is describing significant problems with their family or medical issues that are interfering with their work or causing them distress, you may want to recommend they speak to their boss or Human Resources about taking leave so they can address these issues.** Constant complaints could mean they are not pulling their own weight at work, or it could mean they have lots of challenges in their life right now; either way, let Human Resources sort it out. It's not your place to. Assume good intentions.

11. **Resist the urge to offer advice or to weigh in** on their stories. Responding neutrally then leaving or changing the subject is best.

See also: **Challenge 12: Learn how to have difficult conversations**

Challenge 18: Build allies and friendships at work

Challenge 28: Addressing cultural differences

Take action: Identify how you'll manage an over-disclosing colleague. You can keep it simple ("Gotta go!" while you keep walking) or have a more extensive conversation. But manage it so it stops being a problem.

Challenge 55.
Gossipy colleagues

Gossip is not always bad. Every organization relies on word of mouth to pass information and opportunities along. Good strategic information is invaluable for helping you climb the ladder. Every organization, however, also has a few gossips who seem to revel in negative information about people. These are the people who delight in passing along negative information about other people or stirring up problems. It's important to know the difference between word of mouth information and negative gossip and to not engage with mean-spirited gossip.

1. **Do not engage in negative gossip about people, either to listen or to pass along.**

2. **When people start to gossip, walk away or find something else to do.**

3. **It may be that when you are not present, you will be gossiped about.** Keep the amount of information you share to a minimum to reduce what they can share about you.

4. **Don't feel like you have to spend time with gossip in order not to be the target of negative gossip.**

5. **Create a mantra you can use when people try to pull you into negative gossip,** such as, "Huh. I don't see it that way" or "I don't feel comfortable talking about Brenda like that when she's not here."

6. **Identify someone who seems very good at staying out of negative gossip and ask them how they do it.**

7. **Read the book** *No More Team Drama: Ending the Gossip, Cliques, and Other Crap that Damage Workplace Teams* by Joe Mull to get more insight on how to reduce gossip and build relationships (details listed in the For further reading section).

8. **Consider that some people often do know about useful information before others.** Consider carefully if you choose to engage to trade information with them. Be sure you are acting in accordance with your values and sense of integrity and not engaging in anything negative or that you will regret.

9. **Do not share private information or negative gossip** in areas where you are not sure you are alone (e.g., in a bathroom).

10. **Limit your social media relationship with colleagues who typically engage in negative gossip.** You may want to maximize your social media relationships with people who share useful positive or neutral information.

11. **If you're having a problem at work,** talk to someone you trust outside of work for an external opinion. Don't vent to work colleagues as it might end up in gossip.

12. **If you feel you must engage with some office gossip,** provide very general and non-controversial information and then leave the conversation.

13. **Adjust your expectations about the kind of relationship you can have with overly gossipy colleagues.** Take steps to ensure fairness, but know you might not have the kind of collegial relationship you would like.

14. **If you frequently find yourself on the receiving end of negative gossip,** you may want to consider obtaining help from your boss, a coach, or a therapist who can help you strategize how to change these patterns.

See also: **Challenge 18: Build allies and friendships at work**

Challenge 22: Learn how to say no

Challenge 24: Manage and overcome overwhelm

Take action: Pledge to not contribute to gossip and to share only positive, supportive information about your colleagues.

Part VI.
Managing Up

Challenge 56.
Understanding hierarchy at work and when to go around it

Many organizations have hierarchies and specific offices designed to provide services to employees. The organizational chart and organization policies should identify these offices and what they do.

1. **I use the term *boss* to refer to someone who supervises you or to whom you report for work assignments and other matters.** In most organizations, the person who is the boss is expected to manage the work of the employees and to be the first contact for employees who have concerns, problems, or questions.

2. **The "chain of command" is the formal hierarchy of power and authority in an organization.** Generally instructions and assignments flow down from top leadership to managers to employees and accountability flows upward.

3. **Some organizations have what are called "open-door" policies,** which means that anyone in your chain of command welcomes individuals to talk with them about anything that's on their mind. If you are considering doing this, you might want to first check in with a trusted colleague; some organizations do not respond well when employees actually use the open-door policy!

4. **Your organization likely has an Office of Corporate Compliance.** Compliance is the process of making sure the company and its employees follow appropriate laws, regulations, standards, and ethical practices. This office addresses both external rules (e.g., federal employment law) and internal rules (e.g., company policy).

5. **Human Resources** offices include staffing, professional development, compensation, safety and health, benefits and wellness, and employee and labor relations. Human Resources is the place to go if you have been singled out, bullied, or harassed; if you have personal circumstances that lead to you needing to take time away from work or take medical leave; or if you have questions about benefits such as vacation time or health insurance. Remember, Human Resources are primarily there to ensure the organization is operating within the scope of employment and labor law; they are not employee advocates but can advocate for employees if your interests align with those of the organization.

6. **Larger organizations may have a Diversity, Equity and Inclusion Office** or an **Equal Employment Opportunity** office. These offices are charged with ensuring fairness, inclusion, and equal employment opportunity for all employees and job applicants consistent with federal, state, and local policies. This means that actions must be taken on the basis of merit and without regard to race, color, religion, sex (including pregnancy), age (40 or older), national origin, or disability. Yes, current U.S. law indicates age discrimination only applies to those 40 or older. You would go to this office (which might be within Human Resources) if you feel you are being discriminated against.

7. **If you have a problem, you should go first to your boss.** It's good to ensure your boss is not blindsided or caught unaware of something they could have remedied. If you want to talk with staff in one of these offices, you should let your boss know you'll be away from the job for an appointment.

8. **If your boss is the problem, you can decide to go to your boss's boss or to one of the other parts of the organization.** I recommend first talking with a trusted colleague to identify where to go, as some offices identified may share information you provide with your boss.

9. **Generally, assume that nothing you say at work is confidential unless you are specifically told it is.** Assume that what you say will get back to your boss or to other people, and ensure you present your problems and challenges as diplomatically and objectively as possible.

10. **Find someone outside your organization who is solely invested in your interests** so you can vent, debrief, and strategize. This could include a trusted friend, mentor outside the organization, coach, or therapist.

See also: **Challenge 12: Learn how to have difficult conversations**

Challenge 18: Build allies and friendships at work

Challenge 22: Learn how to say no

Take action: Find the organization chart where you work and make sure you understand what each office does. If not, start asking!

Challenge 57.
Obtaining mentoring from your boss

A mentor is someone who is committed to your growth and professional development. Typically, mentors help you learn what you need to know on the job and how to improve. Sometimes, however, bosses aren't required to mentor, don't like to mentor, aren't aware you need mentoring, or may even be unsupportive of your professional development. Other times, mentorship "just happens" organically. If you have a boss who wants to mentor, that is great, but that is a bonus, not to be expected.

1. **Remember you are responsible** for your own professional development and career growth. When bosses help us, that is wonderful, but ultimately, it's up to us.

2. **Adjust your expectations** to identify ways in which your boss may be supportive of you even if they do not provide the mentorship you would like. It is not reasonable to expect one person to provide all of your mentoring needs.

3. **Read professional publications** in your field so you can learn about current issues and important developments.

4. **Conduct a self-assessment** to understand areas where you feel you need mentoring. Identify if you need skills development, more knowledge, support, or more practice or confidence.

5. **Be alert for opportunities** to learn from your colleagues.

6. **Identify a colleague who is skilled** in an area you want to learn and ask them how they do it. You can also ask for advice on how to improve your skills in that area.

7. **Go to professional conferences** or presentations in your field, so you can keep up with current issues and important developments (and possibly find a mentor!).

8. **Identify professional development programs** in your company or professional association so you can learn what is needed to be successful in your field.

9. **Consider reviewing your company's Human Resources website** or talking with a Human Resources associate about what professional development opportunities might be available. Sign up for newsletters with different organizations in your field to be aware of opportunities.

10. **See the For further reading section** for books about mentoring.

11. **Talk with your boss** about your strengths and areas for improvement. Discuss ways to identify where you might be able to get this support. For example, let your boss know you're interested in a topic and ask if they know someone who could help you with it.

12. **Identify someone other than your boss** who can mentor you on these specific topics.

13. **Consider meeting with others at your level** of experience and seniority and comparing job duties, expectations, needs, etc. You can also develop this meeting into an informal mentoring group. If one doesn't exist, consider starting one.

See also: **Challenge 9: When and how to obtain a mentor**

                    Challenge 18: Build allies and friendships at work

                    Challenge 59: How to respond to your boss's feedback

Take action: What are your skills? What would you like to learn more about? Take a few steps from the tips above to begin putting them into motion.

Challenge 58.
How your boss likes to receive information

Information can be shared verbally or in writing, and at a high or low volume of exchange from each person (and every option in between). The more you understand how your boss likes to receive information, the more effectively you can communicate. Here are some types of communication and ideas for how to find out how your boss likes to receive information.

1. **Regular updates.** I have a Millennial friend who was at a new job for six months and had not yet had a sit-down, face-to-face meeting with her boss (who worked down the hall from her!). Some bosses don't like one-on-one, in-person meetings. Other bosses find them unhelpful; they might not see the value in them, or they don't care to get that close to their staff. If their preferred communication is different from yours, find a way to adjust, which can include meeting with a colleague or your boss's assistant on some issues.

2. **How much information they want.** You might have to do some trial and error to find out how much information your boss wants from you in your updates. Some bosses like to know everything, others don't want to know anything, and others expect you to read their minds. I had a boss once who said at my 6-month review, "You're sharing with me only about 5% of what you're doing, and I'd like you to share only 1%." That was helpful information to have!

3. **Meeting agendas.** Some bosses (like me) are particular about agendas and won't have a meeting without them; others prefer a casual conversation without an agenda. This also depends on seniority. With most bosses, I generally settled on a brief (3-5

item) written agenda to share, and I would take notes if needed on my copy.

4. **What's on your "upcoming" list**. I learned to bring a second document to meetings with a list of all tasks on my plate and upcoming so if they came up in conversation, I could clarify that I hadn't forgotten about them and discuss whether I needed to reprioritize. Sometimes bosses want to know you haven't forgotten and that the tasks are on your radar.

5. **Problems**. Never let your boss be blindsided. That said, some problems can wait until your next face-to-face meeting, others deserve a heads-up email or a request for an interim meeting, and still others require immediate interruption. Your boss's assistant or a colleague who has worked with your boss for a while can help you discern which strategy applies. Once things are calm again, check with your boss about the proper choice and how to handle such problems better in the future. Ideally for every problem you also bring details on what you have already implemented to ameliorate any potential actions your boss might want to take. Make it easy for them to help solve the problem.

6. **Some bosses like to be informed about administrative staff issues,** such as a staff member going on leave or having performance issues. One boss liked to send cards to individuals on leave or meet with people having performance problems. Others preferred for me to handle all of it myself and only bring it up if there was a potential dismissal or legal issue. Use your judgment to make sure your boss who didn't want to know what was happening doesn't undermine you once you've made hard decisions.

7. **Information you gleaned that might be useful to them**. Sometimes you hear things that might be helpful to your boss, whether gossip, that someone's leaving, or that someone said something nice about them. Consider sharing this information strategically (and verbally, so there's no paper trail to follow you).

8. **Sensitive information.** When in doubt, convey sensitive information only verbally and face-to-face. Be aware that in case of legal issues, it might make sense to have counsel present so the information is protected under privilege. I have been in situations where we would discuss a situation under legal privilege and I would draft an email to send through official channels. Emails that cc counsel also are protected under privilege.

9. **Requests for advice.** Learn how your boss likes to give advice. I worked for bosses who loved when I brought them challenging situations. They enjoyed waxing eloquent about possibilities and opportunities, and we could strategize together. Depending on your boss's style, asking for advice occasionally can help them feel valued and improve your relationship with them.

10. **You're leaving.** Definitely tell your boss before you tell anyone else. Of course, there are sensitivities about timing, but by the time any new employer is going to call for references (if your boss is a reference) or when you get an offer letter (if your boss is not a reference), your boss needs to know. They may be upset, but they'll be less upset than if they are blindsided. In addition, they'll be more likely to give you a positive reference if they've had time to work through their initial response.

See also: **Challenge 17: Understanding your team—including your boss and your staff**

Challenge 56: Understanding hierarchy at work and when to go around it

Challenge 57: Obtaining mentoring/sponsorship from your boss

Take action: What is one step you can take to learn how to better manage your boss?

Challenge 59.
How to respond to your boss's feedback

Good bosses give feedback, and as a manager and leader yourself, you'll need to give feedback to your staff. Learning to respond well to feedback from your boss can help you improve how you give feedback to others.

1. **Listen to the content of their feedback,** not the tone. Some bosses give feedback when they're frustrated and may allow that frustration or even sarcasm to slip into the conversation. Try to identify what the concern is and what you should do instead. Try summarizing what your boss told you to ensure you understand the problem.

2. **Set your defensiveness aside.** None of us likes to be told we're wrong. At the same time, that ego and defensiveness stepping up makes it more difficult for us to understand and rectify the problem.

3. **Acknowledge your part in the problem.** You don't have to take the blame for everything bad that happens at work, but it is important to acknowledge anything you did that could have led to the problem—for example, not following up in a timely manner or making an error in a report.

4. **If you disagree with your supervisor's point of view,** seek to understand and state your perspective non-defensively. Arguing your case is not going to be helpful. You may want to state something neutral such as, "I hear what you're saying and I'd like to think this through. Can we discuss it once I've had a chance to digest this information?"

5. **If the feedback is vague,** such as "I'm disappointed," or "That didn't go well," seek to get clarity on what exactly isn't working well, what you could have done differently, or how you can take more responsibility. Sometimes bosses say comments like that *to* you that aren't really *about* you.

6. **It's ok if you don't get top scores on performance reviews all the time**—it doesn't mean you're a failure. You can, of course, ask how you can improve and what it would take to be considered "excellent."

7. **Time is on your side.** You may be able to address the most important parts of the feedback and set other parts aside to address later (or to consider whether you even want to address them).

8. **Consider what help you can get from others** to assist you in addressing the feedback. Would it help to chat with a close colleague, a friend outside of work, or a mentor to understand more about your boss's feedback? It could also be helpful to get another perspective on your behavior or performance, such as from a colleague.

9. **Ask what else you can do to improve your performance.** Repeat back to your boss your understanding of their recommendations on what you can do better. Take notes if you can to help you remember.

10. **Consider what you are willing to do to change.** If you are not in agreement with the boss's feedback or are not willing to change, consider what might be possible. Ultimately, if you can't come to an agreement, you may want to consider a different position or company.

See also: **Challenge 12: Learn how to have difficult conversations**

                 Challenge 13: Set professional goals

                 Challenge 56: Understanding hierarchy at work and when to go around it

Take action: When have you responded poorly to a boss's feedback? When has someone responded poorly to your feedback? What can you do as a manager and leader to facilitate positive response to feedback?

Challenge 60.
Boss doesn't lead

If you have a boss who wants to be liked or a hands-off, distant boss who doesn't support you, you can have a hard time getting *your* work done. Though you're not responsible for fixing your boss, you may find some ways to help work around their lack of leadership.

1. **Be aware that not all bosses are successful leaders.** Identify what you are able to learn from this job and this boss.

2. **Identify what your boss does well.** Remind yourself of this when they're doing something you don't think is particularly skillful.

3. **Be careful to not usurp your boss's authority,** even if they are not using it well. That will only create more problems for you.

4. **Do not confront your boss on what you perceive to be their lack of leadership.** That is not likely to go well. Know that if you are seeing your boss's challenges, other people probably see it as well, even if they can't say anything to you. You are not alone.

5. **Identify job duties that do not rely on your boss and focus on those.**

6. **Review your short-term or long-term plan** and identify how your boss may be able to teach you or help you despite not leading much.

7. **Observe how other people work with this boss** and how they interact.

8. **Consider providing suggestions.** "I found a few possible solutions to this problem. What do you think?"

9. **Talk to someone you trust outside of your team** for perspective on how to work with your boss. Be very diplomatic and stay away from gossip. You don't want your complaints to get back to your boss in a negative way. It often helps to ask someone for advice about the challenge, rather than starting with a complaint. Make sure to have alternate explanations. For example, "I'm wondering if you could help me with a problem. I am working on a project and not getting much guidance from my boss. I know they're really busy, but I'm not sure how to address this. What do you suggest?"

10. **Identify someone who works well with your boss** (or at least who works successfully with them!) and ask them for suggestions.

11. **Remember you are responsible for yourself, your staff, and your work.** You may try to protect your boss or your team, but you are not responsible for your boss's approach to work. Be careful how you invest your energy.

12. **Identify what is bothering you about your boss not leading.** If it's a principle (such as, they are getting paid to lead!) you may want to consider letting the principle go for a while and address the day-to-day challenges that affect you.

13. **Make sure to get an answer from your boss before you leave the room.** Finish the conversations by asking, "I'll get started with this, okay?" or "I want to confirm you're okay to move it forward."

14. **Adjust your expectations** about the kind of relationship you can have with your boss and the kind of guidance they can give you. Take steps to improve the process so you can do your work but know you might not have the kind of mentoring relationship you would like.

15. **Consider where the lack of leadership affects you the most** (meetings, professional development, etc.) and address each topic separately with your boss.

16. You may want to consider obtaining a coach who can help you through this challenge.

See also: **Challenge 9: When and how to obtain a mentor**

Challenge 13: Set professional goals

Challenge 58: How your boss likes to receive information

Challenge 80: Knowing when it's time to move on

Take action: What is one thing you can do to learn and grow, regardless of whether your boss ever leads?

Challenge 61.
Boss gives preferential treatment to others

It can come to you like a punch in the gut: you find out a colleague doing the same work has been getting paid more than you or getting plum assignments that you weren't even invited to consider. Sometimes a person more junior to you is hired at a higher rate—to be your boss! These situations shouldn't happen, and yet they do. While you're steaming about the unfairness, here are some practical suggestions.

1. **Take a deep breath and don't say anything you'll regret later.** Even though it seems unfair, you don't have all the facts. Better to figure out what is happening first and provide a reasoned response. Losing your cool only makes you look bad.

2. **See if there are patterns you can identify.** Are the people getting preferential treatment older, the boss's friends, something else? Try to sleuth out a counterfactual: What else could possibly explain this situation?

3. **Consider talking with your boss about the perceived inequality.** Keep the focus on the perception, and ask politely for an explanation. For example, you could say, "I noticed the last three business trips went to Pat. Can you help me understand how you make decisions on who gets to go on trips? I'm interested in traveling as well."

4. **If you really want to push the issue more, you can ask the question in a group meeting.** This strategy has risks, can irritate your boss, and may make it less likely you will get what you want. If you decide to address it in a meeting, have pre-conversations with others who will be there and ensure you have allies who will speak up about the issue so you are not alone in your concern.

5. **If there is a salary issue or something that may not be in your boss's direct control, consider going to Human Resources to ask the question.** Present yourself as curious, not livid. For example, "I happened to find out that there are some significant discrepancies in salary among us coders. Could you help me understand how salaries are determined, and why they are so different when we are doing the same job?" Do not let the other person take the conversation into how you found this information. If they ask about that, say, "Could you confirm whether the discrepancies I'm presenting to you are real? That's more important than how the information came to me." Ideally, they will offer to review salaries and conduct an equity adjustment.

6. **You may want to contact a lawyer** if you are not getting information from Human Resources or your boss. Remember, Human Resources are not primarily employee advocates, but they can assist you in many situations, especially if your interests align with those of the organization. A lawyer can help you understand your options and let you know the likelihood that you will receive an outcome you desire. If you need to find a lawyer, contact a local university law school for an inexpensive or low-cost referral or Google "best employment lawyer" with the name of your town and call to ask for a free consultation.

7. **Some industries have salary information available.** Contact your trade organization (anonymously if you want) to ask about where to find average salaries for your field. This is a great topic to discuss with a mentor or trusted colleague. Present your observations and ask how they would proceed. Keep in mind you can win the battle and lose the war—consider the longer-term consequences and whether those are worth it.

8. **Sometimes things aren't fair.** It's wrong and awful and you can't fix it. If this is one of those situations, try to find a way to cope—whether it's leaving the job, moving to another work team, continuing to work toward equity, or accepting things as they are.

9. **Adjust your expectations** about the kind of relationship you can have with your boss, and the kind of guidance they can give you. Take steps to increase fairness, but know you might not have the kind of mentoring relationship you would like.

10. **Remember the importance of equity and ensure you are being fair to others** as you advance at work and have more power or employees. Stand up for staff who are climbing the ladder after you.

See also: **Challenge 9: When and how to obtain a mentor**

                Challenge 10: When and how to obtain a career coach

                Challenge 13: Set professional goals

                Challenge 18: Build allies and friendships at work

Take action: If you feel something is unfair, examine the evidence, ask questions, and decide how to proceed. Do something about it or let it go if at all possible.

Challenge 62.
Boss bullies or undermines you

Bullies aren't only for grade school: Some people never grow out of bullying others. Sometimes your boss may say they support you in private and then in public they undermine you by not giving you proper credit, blaming you for problems, or suggesting indirectly that you are not good at your job. You don't have to put up with bullying or undermining!

1. **Clarify what is happening**: Does it directly affect your work? Is it about your work? Is it about your personal life (beliefs, appearance, religion, sexual orientation, race, gender, age, or gender presentation)? This could determine the way you need to deal with it. Generally bullying related to gender, race, and religion could be considered unlawful harassment at work, whereas other kinds of bullying may not be.

2. **Consider talking with your boss** about the organization's and their perspectives on civility and courtesy generally to see if they have self-awareness and will be open to the conversation.

3. Read *The Asshole Survival Guide: How to Deal with People who Treat you Like Dirt* by Robert Sutton (details listed in the For further reading section).

4. **Have a discussion with your boss about your perceptions of the situation** when a bullying or undermining situation happens. Identify what you observed and ask for their perspective, such as by saying, "It seemed like this was intentional; can you help me understand what happened?" Or, if your boss asked you to lead a project and then identified someone else as the lead in public, a casual way to address would be, "I was surprised you said Juan is

the lead of this project in [meeting] when last week you asked me to lead it. Can you help me understand?" Most people will respond kindly and attempt to make the situation better. If they don't, that raises a big red flag.

5. **Remember, it is a reflection on your boss, not on you, if you are bullied or undermined.**

6. **Document incidents of bullying or undermining,** even if it's only in your own note log. Consider emailing notes to yourself so you have a time/date stamp.

7. **Observe the environment where you work to identify if undermining is a common and accepted occurrence** or whether it is generally discouraged. If it is a common and accepted occurrence, consider whether this is the right work environment for you.

8. **Consider what your boss's motive might be**—is it personal to them, are they threatened by you, or is this how they behave? Understanding their motives may help you understand how to counter them and protect yourself.

9. **Do not give them any more information about yourself,** your feelings, or your inner life so they have less information to use against you. Consider whether it may make sense to limit your public expressions of disappointment or hurt. Sometimes it is better to not give people like this the satisfaction.

10. **Consider if you want to respond and stand up for yourself.** There are positive and negative aspects for each option.

11. **Consider talking with appropriate individuals** such as people in your chain of command, Human Resources, or Corporate Compliance, even anonymously, to identify what steps can be taken.

12. **Identify someone senior to you who works well with your boss** and ask them how they manage when your boss gets upset. Or you

can identify people who previously worked with your boss and ask them for tips on how to manage your boss's moods.

13. **Identify colleagues who can stand up for you.** Sometimes even when you can't defend yourself, someone else can defend you, and then you can defend each other.

14. **Adjust your expectations** about the kind of relationship you can have with your boss, and the kind of support they can give you. Take steps to improve the process so you can do your work but know you might not have the kind of mentoring relationship you would like.

15. **If your efforts aren't working, consider that this may be an unsustainable situation and you may need to seek employment elsewhere.** If it is possible, consider switching groups or teams in your organization so you are not working with the bully or underminer.

16. **If you have a pattern of being bullied,** you may want to consider talking with a therapist about how to break these patterns.

See also: **Challenge 9: When and how to obtain a mentor**

Challenge 10: When and how to obtain a career coach

Challenge 13: Set professional goals

Challenge 18: Build allies and friendships at work

> **Take action: Is this the right job for you? Does this fit in with your goals/dreams? Time is the most precious thing we have; do you want to mend the issue and continue or seek new employment? The choice is always yours.**

Challenge 63.
Boss asks me to do work outside of official duties

Usually job duties are pretty clear, but sometimes bosses reach outside of what's appropriate to ask you to do personal tasks for them. There are very few circumstances in which this is acceptable (such as a job as a personal assistant or possibly if you have a pre-existing relationship), and for most day jobs, these are not okay asks.

1. **Review your job description** to ensure you are clear on what is and is not your role.

2. **Read your organization's policies and standards for professional conduct** to ensure you understand the requirements. If there are special circumstances, such as federal funding or financial regulations that apply, make sure you understand the limits of these.

3. **Observe what others in your organization do** so that you have an understanding of what individuals in your kind of position are expected to do for their bosses or more senior people.

4. **If you disagree with tasks your boss asks you to complete, you have options.** You can let your boss know you feel it is inappropriate. You can let someone else (e.g., Human Resources or the Ombudsman's Office) know you feel it is inappropriate. You could also consider whether this is the position you want.

5. **If the action is illegal or harmful to others, you are well within your rights to not do the action** and to raise a whistleblower complaint.

6. **Identify someone senior to you who works well with your boss and ask them how they manage** when your boss asks them to do extra work.

7. **Identify people who previously worked with your boss and ask them for tips** on how to manage your boss's extracurricular requests.

8. **Ask a trusted colleague about the culture at the company** regarding doing favors/work outside of official duties.

9. **Talk to someone you trust outside of work for an outside opinion.**

10. **You may want to consider obtaining a coach who can help you through this challenge.**

11. **Speak up for yourself within reason.**

See also: **Challenge 9: When and how to obtain a mentor**

Challenge 10: When and how to obtain a career coach

Challenge 13: Set professional goals

Challenge 22: Learn how to say no

Take action: If this is happening now, review your job description and take action on the items above. You're not in the wrong if your boundaries are being crossed.

Challenge 64.
Boss insults you in front of others

Ideally, bosses support and praise you in public, and wait for a private meeting to raise criticisms and concerns. Sometimes, however, bosses will say insulting or demeaning things about you in front of others, leaving everyone feeling awkward and you feeling humiliated. What do you do in this situation? Read on . . .

1. **When the insult happens, observe the others to determine if they are also shocked or surprised.** If they are, it will confirm that your feelings and reactions are not misplaced, and these people may become your allies in getting the behavior to stop.

2. **Consider what kind of response may be appropriate at the time,** including perhaps doing nothing. Resist the urge to snap back at your boss in public until you have adequately assessed the situation unless the comment is truly egregious. If it is egregious, sometimes a simple "That's not okay to say" makes your perspective clear.

3. **Talk to your boss in private afterward to let them know that their statement was hurtful and not appropriate.** If possible, engage them in conversation about the statement and determine what is appropriate moving forward.

4. **Document incidents of insults, even if it's only in your own note log.** Consider emailing notes to yourself so you have a time/date stamp and keep emails that reflect the negative situations. These may be helpful if you need to file a complaint.

5. **If the statement is egregious, sexual, or otherwise highly inappropriate,** consider contacting Human Resources immediately, even if anonymously, to report the egregiousness of the situation.

6. **Identify people who can provide perspective on working with your boss;** for example, someone senior to you who works well with your boss or someone who previously worked with your boss. You can say something like, "Sometimes I'm not sure how to interpret what [Boss] is saying, but it doesn't feel good. Can you help me understand your experience with [Boss]?"

7. **Consider asking a trusted friend or colleague for advice** on how to address these situations.

8. **Consider the nature of the work environment.** Some organizations or units within them have a wide tolerance for "joking" behavior that you and others may consider hurtful. If this is the case, consider if this is the right unit/organization for you. At any time, if you are being targeted for your race/ethnicity, gender/gender expression, or religion, that is not acceptable.

9. **If you see this insulting behavior, most likely other people see it too.** Remember you are not alone.

10. **Adjust your expectations about the kind of relationship you can have with your boss.** Take steps to improve the process, but know you might not have the kind of mentoring relationship you would like.

11. **Directly ask a colleague or two to stand up for you in these situations.** If you each stand up for each other, your boss will begin to change (and you will have a better case with the organization that it is a widespread problem).

12. **You may want to consider discussing the situation with a lawyer** if you find it unsafe, excessive, persistent, or personalized. A lawyer represents only you and can help you understand your rights. If you need to find a lawyer, contact a local university law school for an inexpensive or low-cost referral or Google "best employment lawyer" with the name of your town and call to ask for a free consultation.

13. **If this is a persistent pattern that people treat you poorly**, you may want to consider obtaining a coach or therapist who can help you through this challenge.

See also: **Challenge 9: When and how to obtain a mentor**

            Challenge 10: When and how to obtain a career coach

            Challenge 13: Set professional goals

            Challenge 18: Build allies and friendships at work

            Challenge 22: Learn how to say no

Take action: Create your game plan. Pull from suggestions above; what needs to happen first, second, and third? Once you're clear on the direction you're taking, you can begin addressing this.

Challenge 65.
Boss has unreasonable expectations

Bosses are well known for wanting things done immediately. But what do you do when the expectations don't seem to be reasonable for the assignment and for what you can realistically accomplish?

1. **Clarify with your boss what the assignment requires** and ask questions about their expectations and available resources. Are they asking you to be responsible for the completion of the project or only to manage it? Ensure your authority and resources to complete the project is in line with the responsibility you're being asked to take on the project.

2. **Consider whether your boss is trying to challenge you and doesn't realize you are so stressed.** Consider using that opportunity to ask how to manage what you perceive to be expectations that may be too challenging.

3. **Ask a colleague to pitch in to help and offer to repay the favor.** Note this can only be done a few times and is not a long-term solution.

4. **Track your effort on a project through a project management work plan, share with your boss periodically, and ask your boss to help you understand where you might be able to increase your efficiency.** The work plan can clarify a time line and enable you to request additional resources sooner rather than later if tasks need additional time or resources to complete. Having a timeline also allows you to provide options; for example, "If it's just me working on this, I can have it finished in one month. If I have some assistance, we can complete it in two weeks. What would you prefer?" (See resources on project management and work plans listed in the For rurther reading section.)

5. **Let your boss know you want to meet their high expectations and request specific training or advice to help you do so.**

6. **Consider meeting with others at your level of experience and seniority and comparing job duties,** expectations, etc. You can also develop this meeting into an informal mentoring group.

7. **Consider whether you have changed your productivity level.** Sometimes we reprioritize our lives and it impacts work. If this is the case, communicate new boundaries with your boss and see if you can negotiate how to best move forward.

8. **Check with a trusted colleague regarding what expectations would be reasonable for someone with your experience and seniority.** Ask your boss for help on the project, either a colleague to assist or someone more senior to help you understand all the steps so you can complete similar projects yourself next time.

9. **Be careful if you always make near-impossible things happen without resources;** the expectation will be set that you don't need much and that you can always magically pull a rabbit out of a hat. On the other hand, if you can work efficiently, share that information with your boss and colleagues.

10. **Ask around to assess what the norm is in your unit or in your organization.** For example, in most fields it's expected that for professional travel, staff have hotel rooms to themselves and are not expected to share rooms with each other. Clarifying what the norm is will help you make a case to ask for what you need.

11. **Sometimes extending the deadline will give you time to rustle up the resources you need.** Ask if it is a possibility to have more time.

12. **If you are always under-resourced or given near-impossible expectations and your efforts haven't changed this pattern,**

consider if this is the right position or organization for you at this time.

See also: **Challenge 10: When and how to obtain a career coach**

Challenge 18: Build allies and friendships at work

Challenge 22: Learn to say no

Challenge 24: Manage and overcome overwhelm

Take action: Communication is key, wouldn't you agree? Write out a sample email of what you wish to say to your boss about your expectations. Walk away for a bit, let it digest and return with fresh eyes. Where do you need help now? Make a plan and stick with it.

Challenge 66.
Asking for a raise

We all want to get paid more, but raises often seem elusive. Asking your boss for a raise is one of the most stressful conversations to have. But you can do it and be successful.

1. **Proactively communicate accomplishments to your boss over time** so that they have a sense of the good work you have been doing.

2. **Accept that it's normal to ask for a raise sometimes.** It's not greedy or entitled or rude if you are reasonable and don't ask more than once per year.

3. **Consider timing, as some organizations only give raises annually following performance reviews.** An executive I know randomly approves raises, much to the chagrin of their Human Resources staff who are trying to clarify and codify equity. Sometimes it's good to ask for a raise as bosses are preparing next year's budget, or around performance reviews. Check with a trusted colleague or mentor to consider timing.

4. **Identify the circumstances under which raises are given.** If your organization provides raises only after stellar performance reviews, an off-season raise would be challenging for your boss to approve. You may want to ask after a particularly brilliant achievement, or when your boss is in a great mood. Don't ask when your boss is in a bad mood.

5. **Make sure you know your worth.** Research online if you need to or access your organization's publicly available documents for salaries. Many states require their employee salaries to be posted

online, but be aware that could indicate only base salary and not bonuses, benefits, or other perks.

6. **Understand your company's structure for salaries**. Most large U.S.-based companies have a whole set of information detailing for each job title the required education, years of experience, salary range, and advancement opportunity (such as advancing from a bachelor's level assistant to a master's level associate title).

7. **Be sure you can document your accomplishments that support a raise.** Gather your evidence, keeping in mind that often bosses prefer quantitative accomplishments (1% error rate, the lowest in the group) compared to qualitative accomplishments (minimal customer complaints). Make your case on paper first before you go to the boss.

8. **You may want to practice this conversation with a friendly partner beforehand**. Anticipate what your boss might say and practice how you would respond to various comments. Encourage your partner to keep it as realistic as possible; let them know what you are worried or afraid your boss might say, and practice how you respond.

9. **Make sure your reasons for deserving a promotion are professional, not personal**. Do not mention that you are buying a new house or that your mother thinks you should be making more or that you had an addition to the family. These are not relevant to the workplace. Focus on the value you provide and what you bring to the organization. Remember, your boss may have to justify the raise to their bosses; give them enough information to do so successfully.

10. **Clarify to your boss how you will help the organization grow in the future.**

11. **If you have data, such as either from your organization or from the field,** that shows you are being underpaid relative to your skills

and experience, consider discussing a raise as an opportunity to achieve equity with salaries.

12. **If your boss says no to a raise,** ask for how to improve your performance, or what your boss would like to see before they would approve a raise. You can also ask for an alternative, such as additional paid time off or funding to attend a conference.

13. **If your boss says maybe or they will think about it, make sure you clarify the next steps.** You could say something like, "Thanks for your consideration. Would it be okay for me to check back in with you when we meet again in two weeks?"

14. **Be aware that some industries only give raises when you have an offer from another organization and are essentially threatening to leave.** If you go this route, be sure you are willing to leave if you don't get the raise. Work with a trusted colleague, mentor, or coach on timing and framing of these conversations.

See also: **Challenge 10: When and how to obtain a career coach**

Challenge 12: Learn how to have difficult conversations

Challenge 13: Set professional goals

Take action: Identify what resources exist for your field that can help you with identifying what appropriate pay ranges are for your position, skills, and experience. Use online resources to identify your salary compared to others in similar positions.

Challenge 67.
Writing a letter of recommendation

Writing a letter of recommendation can be stressful. Sometimes we don't want to say what we really think of an employee, or we don't want them to leave, or we just don't have time. Not a problem! You can do this.

1. **Know what good letters look like.** Most letters start with an introduction paragraph about what the letter is about and how the writer knows the applicant. For example, "I am writing to provide my strongest recommendation for Alex Smith to enroll in your Master's program in Journalism. I have known Alex for two years; Alex is a staff writer at the *Times*, where I am an editor."

2. **Review the request to ensure you include all components.** This is mostly relevant for academic programs or structured requests, which may ask you to indicate their potential for higher level work, areas that are challenges for them, their strengths and weaknesses, or similar.

3. **Provide examples.** Clear examples that demonstrate that someone is, for example, a quick study or a team player, are appreciated as they help the reader understand who the candidate is.

4. **End letters of recommendation with a closing statement indicating strong approval for the applicant and an offer to contact.** For example, "In sum, Alex has my highest recommendation. Please contact me at [xx] if I can be of further assistance. You will be proud to call Alex a graduate."

5. **Ask the staff to provide you with the information you need.** This can include their resume, information about the educational program/job to which they are applying, and perhaps some talking

points they would like you to emphasize in the letter. For very junior staff, you might want to talk through what you would want to say in a letter. You can ask more senior individuals to draft a letter for you.

6. **Do your best to focus on what will be helpful for the individual while also being diplomatic.** If you're not sure how or if a particular trait should be mentioned, discuss with the staff member.

7. **If the letter is for another job, first discuss the staff leaving, then discuss what should go in the letter.** Thank the staff for the opportunity to work together and provide positive comments such as how much the staff has learned or grown.

8. **Be careful of using "grindstone adjectives."** These are words that focus on your effort (e.g., hard worker) instead of your ability (e.g., brilliant). Studies demonstrate letters of recommendation for women tend to use grindstone adjectives more than letters for men, suggesting that women try hard but men have ability.

9. **If you feel you can't write a positive letter for someone,** let them know as soon as possible. If a letter from their supervisor is required, draft some bullet points and discuss with them. You can say something like, "Given the challenges with your performance while you've been here, I am concerned a letter from me would not be the strongest recommendation for you to get this position. Is there someone else you could ask for a letter?"

10. **Keep a copy of the letter in your files.** It will be helpful for the next letter of recommendation you need. You can use it as a start and update or embellish as needed for the new opportunity!

See also: **Challenge 10: When and how to obtain a career coach**

Challenge 12: Learn how to have difficult conversations

Challenge 13: Set professional goals

Take action: Draft a letter of recommendation you would love someone to write for you. Identify what you want to have accomplished in the next year or two that someone could brag about you and work to achieve those accomplishments.

Part VII.
Strategy and Advanced Politics

Challenge 68.
Create a strong culture

Your company culture is a reflection of what your organization stands for, and as the voice of your business, your employees are key to ensuring that it succeeds. When you provide a work environment that your staff enjoys spending time in, it can help to improve their performance each and every day.

1. **Clarify your purpose.** This could be a combination of the organization's purpose and your individual group's purpose. Ask your staff for feedback on the group's purpose and ensure it is posted and referred to frequently.

2. **What is your vision for your group, division, or company?** There is probably a story about who your group is—the successful department, the underappreciated division, or something else— figure out what that story is and work with your staff on what you want the story to be.

3. **Identify a common language, values, and standards for your group.** For example, is your standard "perfection" or "everyone tries their best" or "just get it done"? Listening to the staff about the current culture and making incremental changes to improve the culture can make an enormous difference over time.

4. **Millennials are leading the way with inclusiveness around gender, race, and sexual orientation, as well as inclusiveness regarding appearance, approach, and communication styles.** And of course, I strongly suggest inclusiveness regarding age and generation. Clarify your stance on inclusiveness and ensure everyone is working from the same playbook.

5. **Focus on what's going well.** Many times managers and leaders focus on goals and problems without acknowledging all of the wonderful work that is ongoing and goals that have already been accomplished. Make sure you acknowledge and appreciate what is going well.

6. **Hold yourself to a high standard.** Your staff are observing you and following your lead.

7. **Repeat your message.** I am a big fan of repeating the same message over and over. You'll know it's sunk in when people start saying it back to you. For example, at one job I said, "Our top goals are regulatory compliance and customer service" over and over and over again. A few months after I started saying that, I was helping a manager problem solve and said, "What are you trying to accomplish?" Her response: "Well, our top goals are regulatory compliance and customer service, so . . . Bingo!"

8. **When you demonstrate that you are interested in the mission and in your staff's success, they will trust you.** Note you can't simply say you're interested in these things, you have to demonstrate it over time. Earn their trust, and they will give you their loyalty.

9. **Identify cultural ambassadors.** Every group has a few people who are superstars. They get their job, they embody the culture, and they are well respected by all. Work with these folks to spread your message whenever possible.

10. **Be honest with your staff, colleagues, and boss.** Diplomacy helps, but it's important for you to be trustworthy.

11. **Communicate and share whatever information you can.**

12. **Treat people well.** Respect goes a long way.

13. **Help orient new staff to the culture,** and help orient staff to move toward the culture you want.

See also: **Challenge 9: When and how to obtain a mentor**

Challenge 10: When and how to obtain a career coach

Challenge 13: Set professional goals

Challenge 18: Build allies and friendships at work

Take action: Ask your colleagues for easy ways to make culture more positive. For example, one colleague has puzzles in the breakroom. People can work on them as they wish, and it provides both a conversation topic and a sense of teamwork!

Challenge 69.
Managing major organizational change

Most managers choose to make some kind of organizational change. Perhaps they decide to implement new processes, or are asked by their bosses to make changes. However you get started, here are some tips to make the process as smooth and impactful as possible.

1. **Read up!** Check out resources such as *Switch* by Chip and Dan Heath, *Leading Exponential Change: Go beyond Agile and Scrum* by Erich R. Bühler, and *Harvard Business Review*'s *10 Must Reads on Change Management* to run even better business transformations.

2. **Communicate with your staff about the need for change and ask for their ideas about what might work so they won't be surprised about an organizational change announcement.** Even if you've been thinking about it for months, they will need some time to adjust.

3. **Ensure you have support from your boss and ideally your boss's boss as well.** If anything goes awry or not as planned, you will need their confirmation that you are on the right track and have their support for the bumpy parts of the road.

4. **If you are leading the change, start early building a team that includes advisory members (who may be outside your group), workers, and supporters.** Ensure roles are defined clearly. Invite the team to share what might not work, or concerns they have. Better to hear them first and be able to deal with them than hear it later.

5. **Plan everything as you get information about the change.** Plan what you would like to happen, and then ask colleagues to comment on what might not work or where things can go wrong.

Update your plan to mitigate these risks. Plan how you'll train people, monitor progress, and communicate with all stakeholders.

6. **Communicate, communicate, communicate! Overcommunicate!** Constantly communicate! Start out by explaining to your team what the problem is that is being addressed, how it's being addressed, and what changes your team will experience. Clarify how success is being defined, what won't change, and the time frame for the change. Communicate with other divisions or groups who may be affected by the project or by your team's work on the project. Throughout the project, reiterate that you appreciate everyone's support/work on the project, and that anyone can come to you at any time with any concerns or questions.

7. **Manage staff resistance.** Not everyone embraces change as much as we do! Even if you are not 100% in support of the change, you can manage resistance by ensuring you have support from your bosses, developing information and tools for managers, and rewarding desired behaviors. Updates on progress can help keep staff—even naysayers—motivated.

8. **Ensure you are getting support from friends and family outside of work.** If you are in a particularly challenging time of the change, ask them for what you need.

9. **Ensure that you are taking care of yourself** physically, by getting enough healthy food, exercise, and sleep to the extent you can.

10. **Stay flexible and positive.** Organizational change rarely happens exactly as planned. Lean on your planning and risk mitigation to help you through challenging spots. You can do this!

11. **You may want to consider obtaining an organizational consultant or coach who can help you through this challenge.** I'm happy to recommend someone—email me at jennifer@leadwithwisdom.com.

See also: **Challenge 12: Learn how to have difficult conversations**

Challenge 13: Set professional goals

Challenge 18: Build allies and friendships at work

Take action: Ask colleagues about major organizational changes they have experienced, from changing financial or information technology systems to a change in leadership. What did they learn? What can you learn from their experiences?

Challenge 70.
Impossible decisions

Impossible decisions are decisions where multiple options seem equally good or equally bad, or where both have good and bad aspects that are different—and seem impossible to navigate! Thankfully, the more you make regular decisions, the better you'll get at impossible decisions. Take a deep breath, get ready to think through things, and read on . . .

1. **Clarify what decision you really have to make and if you have to make it now.** I used to spend a lot of time worrying about making decisions that hadn't actually presented themselves yet! You don't have to choose baby names if you're not expecting, and you don't have to decide how to respond to a job offer you don't actually have. Be mindful of not stressing out about decisions that you don't have to make now.

2. **Try to get as much information as possible about your options and their pros and cons.** It's really hard to make decisions based on hypothetical information (and it's also a waste of time!). You might find that some of your assumptions aren't entirely true or that more options can present themselves.

3. **Even as you get more information, examine the evidence.** Will turning down a job offer mean you'll *never* get another opportunity? Will not asking for a raise now mean the window is shut for *a year*? Sometimes our brains fill in the gaps with anxieties or worst-case scenarios that aren't actually true.

4. **Beware false binaries.** Rarely are decisions so black and white, as in weighing a great job in a town you don't like vs. a job you don't like in a town you love. If you find you're thinking in black and white, search for the gray. It's there!

5. **Consider that many times you have to choose the least worst option**. That can be a good decision too.

6. **Brainstorm out of the box options,** especially options that may initially sound far-fetched or impossible. They're only impossible because they haven't happened yet. And you never know when expanding the parameters of what's possible can help you come up with a creative solution!

7. **If you're highly analytical, identify what you value and rank each option by your values.** For example, you may prioritize protecting junior staff, keeping your own job, or making money. Then you can rank each opportunity by how well it achieves those priorities. Note that every time I've done this, my ranking of these uncovered what I truly wanted, which usually wasn't the top-ranked choice. Sometimes this is a useful exercise to get you thinking differently.

8. **It's natural to sometimes be afraid or anxious, especially about the future**. Physiologically, the bodily experience of fear and anxiety (racing thoughts, pounding heart) are similar to those of excitement. Choose to relabel fear and anxiety as excitement.

9. **Be aware you will often need to make decisions without all of the information**. Practice reflection after decisions to determine what you did well and not as well, what information could have been helpful, and what you learned for next time.

10. **Remember what is in your control and what isn't.** Your decision: in your control. What happens next: not in your control. That gives you freedom.

11. **Talk to a mentor or someone you trust outside of work for an outside opinion on your choices**. They can also help you brainstorm options.

12. **You may want to consider obtaining a coach who can help you through impossible work decisions.**

13. **Consider adjusting your expectations about what "success" means for impossible decisions.** Sometimes it's enough to have learned something, even if you don't accomplish what you set out to do. Don't lower your standards but identify what might be possible.

14. **Boost your confidence in impossible decisions by telling yourself that you can't lose.** No matter what you decide, there will be benefits and challenges. Either you get what you want, or you get experience and a story you can use to help others. As long as you're staying true to your values and not hurting others, you're going in the right direction.

15. **Take it easy on yourself if everything doesn't work out like you planned.** You did the best you could with the information you had at the time, and it was a (possibly painful but definitely educational) opportunity to learn and grow.

See also: Challenge 9: When and how to obtain a mentor

Challenge 10: When and how to obtain a career coach

Challenge 13: Set professional goals

Take action: What seems impossible just hasn't been considered fully yet. Think of an impossible choice you had to make before. What did you learn?

Challenge 71.
Integrating work and life

So many people talk about work-life balance, as if there's a perfect ratio to achieve that will make everything manageable. For most of us, it's a constant process of reassessing and adjusting from month to month, season to season, and after life changes. Being a great manager or leader is NOT incompatible with having a rich life outside of work, including family. How you manage that integration, however, is up to you.

1. **Figure out how far you want to go in your job, as this will affect the decisions you make with regard to integrating work and life.** You may be set on the corner office and chief executive officer. You may prefer a middle management position that pays a decent salary and allows you plenty of time outside work. Or you may be passionate about your job in communications or public affairs that isn't as likely to lead to upper management positions. These choices come with general expectations for availability and free time (including family time). Although there are always exceptions, it's worth considering how much you want to put into work.

2. **Clarify your goals.** Similar to how far you want to go, if you want a full-time job and side hustle and children and competitive weekend sports, you'll need to be more focused on systems and organization than people who want only some of those things. Whatever goals you choose, be mindful of how you can best integrate what you want into the time you have. You can make it work to have lots of travel or lazy weekends, but you'll need to adjust in other areas. These may also adjust over time throughout seasons, kids' ages, or work requirements.

3. **Question work processes and policies that don't allow flexibility.** For example, rigid working hours are likely on their way out for most jobs, but they are important for some positions (e.g., call center). There may be technological opportunities to provide flexibility (such as working a call center from home or using video conferencing).

4. **Perfectionism is the enemy of work-life balance.** Strive for excellence, build in time as needed to make adjustments, and know you have to let some things go. Unless you're a surgeon—then definitely strive for perfection!

5. **When you're off work, be *off work*.** Unplug, don't ruminate about work issues, and find other things to think and talk about.

6. **Prioritize your health,** including exercise, sleep, eating well, meditation, yoga, or other kinds of self-care. It's amazing how much more we can accomplish when we're healthy.

7. **Strive as much as possible to be performance-oriented instead of time-oriented.** This means that you're focused on what you are accomplishing instead of how many hours you're on the job. If your job is time-oriented, see if there are creative ways to meet everyone's goals, such as rotating which faces are present to give others time to work from home, or having an on-call person to answer all immediate concerns so not everyone has to be jumping all day.

8. **Take a hard look at your schedule and identify places for efficiency,** including meetings that can be cut from an hour to a half-hour, or check-ins that can be bimonthly instead of weekly.

9. **If there are time-wasting meetings that require your presence but not your intense focus and attention, bring multitasking work, such as updating your to-do list or outlining a report.**

10. **Adjust your expectations so you are not expecting a perfect work-life balance like you see in the movies,** because that's

not necessarily realistic for your circumstances. Identify what's important to you, and focus on that.

11. **Chitchat and office gossip can be enormous time wasters.** Consider whether your time (and that of your team) is idle gossip versus useful team-building conversations.

See also: **Challenge 13: Set professional goals**

Challenge 18: Build allies and friendships at work

Challenge 22: Learn how to say no

Take action: Start small. Rather than trying to overhaul your whole life at once, take one step toward work-life integration. What step will you try today?

Challenge 72.
Don't see a path through challenge at work

Sometimes your challenge may not be listed here. If that's the case, here are some steps to find information on your particular challenge so you can address it confidently and effectively.

1. **Google the problem to see if anyone has addressed it online and identify who they went to for help.**

2. **Be aware you will often need to make decisions without all of the information.** Practice reflection after decisions to determine what you did well and not as well, what information could have been helpful, and what you learned for next time.

3. **Find online forums related to your problem, such as Reddit.**

4. **Identify a colleague who seems to always know where to go with problems and ask for advice.**

5. **Talk to someone you trust outside of work for an external opinion on the problem.**

6. **Identify a similar problem that may have related solutions;** for example, office friendships gone bad may have some similar solutions to office romances gone bad.

7. **Consider waiting if waiting won't cause irreparable damage;** sometimes problems work themselves out.

8. **Clarify the problem in writing, identify some possible solutions, and then try one.**

9. **Gather some friends for coffee or lunch and ask them to help you brainstorm solutions.**

10. **Consider searching reputable advice columnists,** such as Miss Manners, Alison Green's "Ask a Manager," or Carolyn Hax's "Tell Me About It" for similar problems and solutions.

11. **Identify books with characters who face and overcome significant problems.** Although it might not give you a specific solution, it can increase your confidence that you will be able to deal with this particular problem.

See also: **Challenge 9: When and how to obtain a mentor**

                 Challenge 10: When and how to obtain a career coach

                 Challenge 18: Build allies and friendships at work

Take action: Every challenge has a solution; some are just more elegant than others. What is a challenge you have now that needs a solution? What is one step you can take to work toward a solution?

Part VIII.
Career Challenges

Challenge 73.
Career uncertainty

Although we are all used to a rapidly changing world, sometimes things really speed up in ways that make our career feel even more tenuous. What do you do in these moments? Read on!

1. **Update your resume.** Regardless of how things end up, updating your resume will remind you of your value and experiences, and will make you more prepared if you end up needing to look for work.

2. **If you are so moved, update your *life* resume.** I started one years ago to remind myself of what I've experienced outside of work and to help me keep perspective on what's important in my life. I include important relationships, adventures, losses, and achievements and update it periodically. Try it! This will also remind you that work is but one part of who you are and that you have many aspects of who you are that will be fine, even with some career uncertainty.

3. **Identify immediate concerns** such as your family's income needs, possible budget adjustments, how long it might take to retrain or find another similar position, and what each person's role can be to help everyone emerge stronger. If you are a solo act, consider what resources you have to buffer you financially and emotionally during this period of uncertainty.

4. **Practice holding opposing ideas in your head:** This could follow the path to the left, or it could follow the path to the right, and either way would be okay.

5. **Meditation will help you center yourself and increase perspective.** If you haven't meditated before, there's no time like the present to start!

6. **Remember your career is your responsibility.** Regardless of what happens, you have skills and experiences to find your way. And you have the ability to learn more skills if you want!

7. **Learn breathing exercises to increase your calm** when you're feeling distressed or even when you're not.

8. **Adjust your expectations for certainty.** Many times, I've experienced career uncertainty, whether externally (job situation changes) or internally (I'm not sure what I want). Know you can work through it.

9. **Consider working with a career placement firm** to discuss options for moving forward. If nothing else, they can review your resume and provide feedback.

10. **You may want to consider obtaining a coach** who can help you through potential career change and to help you understand your options better.

See also: **Challenge 9: When and how to obtain a mentor**

Challenge 10: When and how to obtain a career coach

Challenge 13: Set professional goals

Take action: What do you want? So much of our decisions come down to what we'd like to have happen, and then we can work backward from there to identify steps to move in that direction.

Challenge 74.
Career is stalled

Are you stuck? Do you feel like you may retire or die in your current career choice? If so, your career may be stalled and you are not sure how to move forward. Read on for some tips on how to take control of your career.

1. **Consider what you would like to do with your life and work toward creating a vision of what you would like.**

2. **Identify someone who seems happy in their work and ask them what brings them satisfaction.** You might be surprised!

3. **Update your resume or CV.** Regardless of how things end up, updating your resume will remind you of your value and experiences, and will make you more prepared if you end up needing to look for work.

4. **If you are considering a major change of career, read** *What Color is Your Parachute?* to help you think through steps of career transition.

5. **Consider working with a career placement firm to discuss options for moving forward.**

6. **Ask your boss for a challenging assignment or take on a challenge on your own.** This could be something directly associated with work or something adjunct to work (like starting a charity drive at work).

7. **Take an in-person class or seminar or online course about a component of your career and notice if you can feel excitement**

about your career. If so, cultivate that excitement. If not, try something else.

8. **Identify career trajectories that are typical for people in your line of work and see how you compare.** Remember there are often atypical trajectories that might be even more interesting!

9. **Consider adjusting your expectations around the meaning of "stalled career."** Maybe your career isn't stalled at all: maybe you're recovering from a difficult year, or building your strengths for a big move, or taking some time to decide what's next. Interpreting it more positively can help you be more successful in working through it.

10. **Identify someone in your field who is 5 or 10 years more senior than you** and ask them about their career path and decisions they made to get there. Ask them for advice.

11. **Talk to someone you trust outside of work for an outside opinion.**

12. **You may want to consider obtaining a coach who can help you through restarting your career.**

See also: **Challenge 9: When and how to obtain a mentor**

Challenge 10: When and how to obtain a career coach

Challenge 13: Set professional goals

Take action: What is one thing you can do differently that will open a new door? Meeting someone new? Doing something differently? Even taking a different path to work can all set off chain reactions to create something new.

Challenge 75.
Need new ideas for career

Sometimes you just get in a funk and you're not sure what to do next. Should you stay in your current position? Apply for a promotion? Sell your stuff and sail around the world? So many options!

1. **If you're not sure what advancement opportunities there are in your current company, do some sleuthing.** Find the organizational chart to see what kinds of departments and roles there are in the company, review the organization's website, and talk to people about what they do and how they got to their current role.

2. **If you are considering a major change of career,** read *What Color is Your Parachute?* to help you think through steps of career transition. See the For further reading section.

3. **Identify the top companies in your field and review their websites and publicly available information.** See whose jobs look interesting and find out more about them. Reach out to people on LinkedIn or through other social media to have a brief conversation about their career path, what they like about their job, what they don't like, and any advice.

4. **Identify people with interesting careers and consider asking them to coffee to have a brief informational interview about their career path and current satisfaction/dissatisfaction.**

5. **Update your resume or CV.** Regardless of how things end up, updating your resume will remind you of your value and experiences, and will make you more prepared if you end up needing to look for work.

6. **There are lists of job titles available online.** When I first had to write an essay on "What I wanted to be when I grew up" for a scholarship, I went to one of these lists (in a book at the time) and started the process of elimination. Although I would take more time if I had it to do over again, it served me well and helped me write the essay, get the scholarship, and get into my current career!

7. **There are also surveys available online that can help you identify the kinds of careers you might be interested** in based on your interests and skills. Search online for "career interest inventory."

8. **Remember you are responsible for your career, and life is long. You will figure this out.**

9. **Career choices are not always rational or logical decisions.** Keeping your eyes and ears open, talking with people about what you're looking for (such as, "I'm just starting to think about what else might be out there, careerwise") and intentionally noticing what kinds of work people are doing will help you move in the right direction.

10. **You may want to consider obtaining a coach or working with a recruitment consultant who can help you through career planning.**

See also: **Challenge 9: When and how to obtain a mentor**

Challenge 10: When and how to obtain a career coach

Challenge 13: Set professional goals

Take action: What's one step you can take today to help you think more creatively about your career options?

Challenge 76.
Afraid to take next career step

We all have moments of paralysis—we don't want to take a step for fear it's the wrong one. You can work through this, and here's how.

1. **Review your resume to identify all of the work experience you have,** all of the chances you've taken, and how much you've grown. That can help increase your confidence to move forward.

2. **Clarify your vision.** What is the difference you'd like to make in the world? What strengths do you bring to the table? How would you like to feel about your career? Even if all you can clarify is "I'd like to be excited about my work," that's a good start. The more clarity you can find, the closer you can get to achieving your vision.

3. **Identify what your fears are about.** You may be reluctant to leave an organization that has felt like home, go apply for a promotion that would leave your peers behind, or to switch careers and risk financial penalties. If your fears are primarily realistic/reality based, look into how you can address them.

4. **In addition to reality-based fears, there may be other, deeper fears,** such as "Who am I to reach for more?" or "This is as good as it gets," or "If I reach further and fail, it will be all my fault." Those fears may take more work, such as with a close friend or therapist. Still, addressing them is important to move forward. I like to consider Helen Keller's statement, "Life is either a daring adventure or nothing at all" to encourage me to take risks.

5. **As you get to know your fears, don't try to deny or eliminate them immediately.** Let them exist. While this may seem counterintuitive, your fears are there for a reason and can help you learn and grow. Fear is often simply an indicator that you care

about something and that you're facing the unknown. Tolerating the anxiety of having those fears helps you get more comfortable with the discomfort so you can make a solid decision that takes your fears into account but doesn't let them dictate your actions.

6. **Talk with people who have made daring career moves.** Ask them how they knew it was time to make a leap, how they prepared, what they regret, and how it worked out. Ask for advice if it's appropriate. Most people are happy to share their experiences with you and want to be helpful.

7. **Read about people who have taken risks.** There are a number of books on the topic, including Po Bronson's *What Should I Do With My Life?* and Jeremy Scott's *Women Who Dared.*

8. **If you are considering a major change of career,** read *What Color is Your Parachute?* to help you think through steps of career transition. See the For further reading section.

9. **It's natural to sometimes be afraid or anxious, especially about the future.** Physiologically, the bodily experience of fear and anxiety (racing thoughts, pounding heart) are similar to those of excitement. Choose to relabel fear and anxiety as excitement.

10. **Conduct informational interviews with people in roles you find interesting.** Ask for 20 minutes of their time and prepare questions such as, "How did you get into this role?" "What do you like about leading?" "What advice do you have?" Be sure to thank them, in writing if possible.

11. **Adjust your expectations of what a "next step" is.** A next step doesn't have to be a new job in a new field; a perfectly fine next step is learning more information or talking to people or trying any of the suggestions listed here. Give yourself credit for small steps as well as big steps! It's all part of the process.

12. **If you're considering starting a side hustle or becoming an entrepreneur,** there are many resources for that work as well,

including Pamela Slim's *Escape from Cubicle Nation* and David Heinemeier Hansson and Jason Fried's *Rework*.

13. **You may want to consider obtaining a coach who can help you through career transitions.**

See also: **Challenge 9: When and how to obtain a mentor**

   Challenge 10: When and how to obtain a career coach

   Challenge 13: Set professional goals

   Challenge 22: Learn how to say no

Take action: Fear is letting us know we need to consider something. What is it you need to consider? Write down your fears and start addressing them one by one.

Challenge 77.
Dealing with success

What happens when you're doing really well? Sometimes we can get pushback from others who are not as successful, feel frustrated we're not moving faster, or wonder, "Now what?" Here are some ideas to keep you zooming ahead!

1. **Acknowledge your successes to yourself and your friends and family.** Regardless of how others act at work—praising you, celebrating you, ignoring you—it's important for you to note your successes. If needed, deliberately seek out someone you know will be impressed with your achievements.

2. **Realize that after a success, you might feel negative.** It's common to feel exhausted, aimless, or bored or to have doubts about your effectiveness. Work with the negativity to find ways to be more positive, such as by taking a break, changing what you normally do (such as teaching others), or finding a new goal to aim for.

3. **Consider how you are different after the success**—both good and bad. Getting a promotion, for example, can make you feel really good about yourself, and it can also mean the loss of friends, a change in your relationship with colleagues, or guilt in leaving others behind. Continue to cultivate positive relationships with your boss, coworkers, staff, mentors, and others.

4. **Keep seeking feedback on how to be more effective.** Be careful when asking for feedback that you don't present as weak or lacking confidence. Also, if you're open to asking for feedback, make sure you're also open to being willing to change.

5. **Give to others.** As you learn, grow, and achieve success, it's important to "lift as you climb." This means you're always helping

others by sharing what you know, who you know, and how you got there. Being generous can also mean being judicious; you aren't obligated to continue to give to someone who is resentful, doesn't follow up, or undermines you.

6. **Continue to broaden your experience and perspective**. Learn about other departments at the company, other companies or individuals who do similar work, vendors, customers, products, and everything else you can.

7. **Review the skills needed to be a good manager or leader** (See Challenge 3) and your technical skills (such as finance, information technology, or design). Create a plan for how to keep learning.

8. **Talk with people 5-10 years ahead of you** in your field to share your successes and brainstorm next steps and opportunities.

9. **Ask a trusted colleague and a friend outside of work to keep you in check** if you start getting arrogant about your success. These may be difficult conversations, but they're so important!

10. **Ask your boss to reflect on what you need to learn**, such as negotiation, delegation, technical skills, or something else. Request their help on stretch goals and challenging assignments.

See also: **Challenge 13: Set professional goals**

Challenge 18: Build allies and friendships at work

Take action: Now that you've achieved success, what are your next goals? Dream big!

Challenge 78.
Learning from failure

Randy Pausch, an educator who delivered his famous "Last Lecture" while he had terminal cancer, said, "Experience is what we get when we don't get what we want." Failure happens to the best of us. Sometimes it's because of our own personal inadequacies, sometimes because a company fails and takes us with it, or sometimes we misjudge situations. Learning from failure can help us turn challenges into something positive.

1. **Understand what happened**. Without blame, identify what happened and how you thought, felt, and responded. Critically evaluate whether any other explanations might be possible for what happened, and how your responses might have misread the situation, missed the mark, or responded too forcefully.

2. **Take a break if you can**. Whether it's an evening, a weekend, or a weeklong vacation away from work, try to let yourself not think about the situation for a little while. Doing something that can keep you out of your thoughts, such as running, listening to music, going for a strenuous walk, sleeping, or crafts, can allow your brain time to process everything while you're focused elsewhere.

3. **If it's possible, ask for feedback on the failure**, such as why you weren't selected for a job or why your product wasn't chosen for production, or why you were laid off. Sometimes people will be honest with you. It's important to accept what they are saying to you without arguing back, even if you don't agree with it.

4. **Be aware that sometimes failure was inevitable**: The company had selected their top candidate before you even interviewed, your boss undermined you, or the market crashed at the wrong time for

you to be successful. Inevitability doesn't mean you can't still learn from it.

5. **Recognize failure as the loss that it is.** If you weren't promoted, were laid off, or your ideas weren't accepted, that can really hurt because something (even if only your expectation of success) was taken away. If you have had other experiences in your life of loss or abandonment, consider how you might be responding to this loss with regard to those other experiences. Give yourself time to adjust and mourn if needed and be sure you don't take out your frustration on others.

6. **One failure doesn't mean you're doomed.** Even if you didn't accomplish what you wanted, you can still grow from the experience professionally and personally, and you might also have gained visibility or kudos from others for how you shot for the stars or handled the situation.

7. **Consider whether there are steps you can take to be more successful next time.** For example, maybe you perform well in your job, but you aren't demonstrating initiative or self-improvement. Perhaps you don't really like your job and your approach led people to think you're not interested in advancement. There are opportunities to consider how you are viewed by others and to actively work to change their perspectives.

8. **If you have strong technical skills, consider whether there are behavioral issues that could be affecting your ability to be successful.** The more you rise in an organization, the more abrasiveness, passivity, lack of discipline, or inability to set challenging goals will hold you back.

9. **If you are really beating yourself up, adjust your understanding of the word *failure*.** Find ways in which you did at least part of the process well, identify what you learned, and find the silver lining. You could also try using a different word altogether: you either succeed, or you have a wonderful learning opportunity!

10. **Consider whether different styles or something more pernicious might be at play.** Some men still have problems with assertive women and vice versa, some older people have issues with Millennials because of their age and vice versa, and many bigots still discriminate on the basis of race, ethnicity, or sexual orientation. If you think this might be the case, consider discussing it with a trusted colleague, contacting Human Resources if you have it available, and considering your next steps carefully.

11. **If you feel like you are not being seen for your strengths and skills, talk with someone such as your boss to identify how you are being seen.** This can be a difficult conversation, and it will be important to accept feedback without getting angry.

See also: **Challenge 9: When and how to obtain a mentor**

   Challenge 24: Manage and overcome overwhelm

   Challenge 25: Commit to continuous self-improvement

Take action: Babies don't refuse to try when they're learning to walk. They keep going until they figure it out. What is a failure you experienced that made you stronger or that taught you an important lesson? How can that be helpful now?

Challenge 79.
About to get terminated

Everyone in your workplace is on edge with nervous looks and talks of budget cuts and downsizing. Or your boss puts you on a performance improvement plan and lets you know you need to shape up. Either way, if you think you are about to get terminated, here are some things you can do to make a tough situation a little easier.

1. **Update your resume and potential references.** Regardless of how things end up, updating your resume will remind you of your value and experiences, and will make you more prepared if you end up needing to look for work.

2. **Take a look at your personal financial situation** and implement cost savings if you can or if you need to, just in case.

3. **If you might get terminated due to performance,** make sure you understand the company's rules about managing performance. Usually you'll be given a chance to improve. If you want to stay at the company, let them know you want to improve and ask for the help you need.

4. **Keep up with networking.** If layoffs are looming over everyone, it's a good opportunity to meet with colleagues in your organization and outside of it to keep your network active. Let people outside your organization know if you're starting to look for other options, but there's no need to share if you're feeling desperate.

5. **Breathe.** This too shall pass. Whatever happens, you are resilient, resourceful, and you have options. No need to panic.

6. **Remember it's almost always better to know the truth than to worry about what might happen next.**

7. **You may want to attend to your personal effects.** If you have personal information on your work phone or laptop or computer, go ahead and delete it. Take home any personal files you may have been storing at work. Backup your contacts or any other information you are allowed to remove in case you get terminated.

8. **Don't burn bridges.** Even if you don't agree with the circumstances of how your boss or company handles the termination, be diplomatic.

9. **Be careful sending emails from work.** Your employer has the right to review your work email or may even allow a successor access to your work email so they can keep up with customers or meetings.

10. **Consider talking with your boss about the current situation at your organization.** You may want to ask directly whether you are likely to be terminated (such as if there are rumors of upcoming layoffs). Be aware your boss may not be able to answer you directly.

11. **Consider what your employer might offer if you are terminated,** including health insurance past your termination date, severance pay, how your departure is characterized in your personnel file, how your termination will be referred to when references call, outplacement services, vacation hours payout, and eligibility for unemployment.

12. **You may want to consider obtaining a coach who can help you through a career transition.**

See also: **Challenge 9: When and how to obtain a mentor**

Challenge 10: When and how to obtain a career coach

Challenge 24: Manage and overcome overwhelm

Challenge 25: Commit to continuous self-improvement

Take action: Set your emotions aside and make a list of what you need to do if you are terminated. You can return to emotions later, and the plan will help you now.

Challenge 80.
Knowing when it's time to move on

One of the most common questions I get asked in my consulting and coaching business is "How do I know when it's time to move on?" While it's an entirely individual decision, here are some things to consider.

1. **Have you learned what you can in this job?** Although there's always more to learn, if you're reaching your point of diminishing returns (where you're not continuing to learn new stuff), it might be time to look for something else that will challenge you more.

2. **Are you at a point in your life where you can spend a few months to a year focusing on looking for another position?** Or a financial place where you can leave this job, take a few months off, and look for something else? Realistically, what is your flexibility in looking for a new job?

3. **Consider your big goals.** What do you want to do with your life? Is there a way this job (or having a job) can help you pursue those goals, even if it isn't ideal? If you feel like what you're working toward at your job isn't important or worthwhile, it's okay to move on to a position where you feel like you're making a positive difference.

4. **Consider your values.** If you're working in a field or a role that is no longer compatible with your values, it might be time to move on. When it emerged that a company I was working for was doing some shady business, it helped spur me on to find another opportunity.

5. **You are not under any obligation to try everything you can to make a difficult situation work.** You can leave because you're

unhappy, or bored, or for no reason at all. Really. You'll want to think through your decisions and next steps and what you want, but it's perfectly fine to leave.

6. **Some situations make it easy to walk:** harassment, unethical behavior, narcissistic boss. Those are good signs it's time to get out.

7. **It's useful to get opinions from trusted mentors or friends about whether you should leave.** Recognize that everyone has their own anxieties and strengths about moving on: some people get very nervous when thinking about leaving and try to pass that on to you by telling you awful stories of how you won't make it, or you're safer to stay here, or "people will think" poorly of you. Use what is useful for you, and don't take on their anxieties.

8. **Similarly, be kind with people who get upset about you moving on.** It's about them, not you.

9. **Allow time for reflection.** At least once a week, take some time to review what you've learned and ensure you're on the right track. Identify what you really enjoy about your job and what you don't care for. Ideally, you want a job that has lots of what you enjoy and a minimal amount of what you don't care for. How can you make that happen?

10. **Plan your future mindfully and take advantage of unexpected opportunities to learn and grow.** Chance favors the prepared mind.

See also: **Challenge 9: When and how to obtain a mentor**

Challenge 24: Manage and overcome overwhelm

Challenge 25: Commit to continuous self-improvement

Take action: Think about what, if anything, has led you to move on in the past? Where do you draw the line?

Challenge 81.
Looking for a job when you have a job

Looking for a job when you have a job can be hard to do because you may not want your current job to know you are looking: they might get upset, let you go, or otherwise not react favorably.

1. **Update your resume.** Regardless of how things end up, updating your resume will remind you of your value and experiences, and will make you more prepared if you end up needing to look for work.

2. **Conduct informational interviews with people in roles you find interesting.** Ask for 20 minutes of their time and prepare questions such as, How did you get into this role? What do you like about leading? What advice do you have? Be sure to thank them, in writing if possible.

3. **Look for jobs online from a source that is not on your company's network.** Some companies monitor your online time at work, and that would not be a good look.

4. **As you are getting started, come up with a story about why you are leaving that is accurate, authentic, and diplomatic.** That way, if you're surprised by someone who finds out you're leaving, you can have a response that is appropriate and you won't have to stammer or feel embarrassed. Always make your story positive—not "My boss stinks here," but "I'm looking for more opportunities to grow." Even if you might not feel like being polite, your diplomacy will pay off. Remember that as a manager/leader, you're also setting an example for your staff.

5. **As you start to interview, plan interviews to not interfere with your current responsibilities.** Take time off if you have to. Note

that if you take the morning off and come into work in a suit, people will recognize if that's different from your normal attire.

6. **Keep it to yourself or share only with someone you absolutely trust.** If it gets out it could cause some issues around your office.

7. **Consider what it will be like to move on.** Are there projects you want to finish before you go? If so, get moving on them. Are there staff you need to train to take on some of your responsibilities? If so, start training (you don't have to tell them you're leaving; tell them you want to support their professional development).

8. **Don't leave your team hanging.** If there's a big project coming up that you are an essential part of, consider how to manage so your team doesn't get stuck holding the bag.

9. **Consider how and when you'd like to tell people you are moving on.** You may want to give some people more of a heads-up that you're leaving. Generally you should give your boss informal notice before you announce it to your team, department, or company. Other people you may want to tell in person individually, in person in a group, by phone, or by email or text. Make a list if it's a lot of people!

10. **Ensure you're set up for references that do not include your current employer or coworkers unless they already know you're leaving and unless you're sure they will give you a positive review.** You can ask your prospective employer to be discreet, but at some point they will likely have to contact your current employer.

See also: **Challenge 9: When and how to obtain a mentor**

Challenge 25: Commit to continuous self-improvement

Challenge 67: Writing a letter of recommendation

Take action: What is your first step if you want to start looking for a job? Start it now!

Challenge 82.
Moving on

Leaving a job is often challenging, and it's even more complicated when you have staff you'll leave behind. Once you've decided to make the leap, here are some ideas for how you can make the transition as smoothly as possible.

1. **Talk with people who have made daring career moves.** Ask them how they knew it was time to make a leap, how they prepared, what they regret, and how it worked out. Ask for advice if it's appropriate.

2. **Prepare what you will say if people find out about your departure.** Come up with a statement that is authentic to who you are and that doesn't put down your employer, boss, or other staff at the organization where you were. If you don't want to share where you're going next, you don't have to, but know people will ask and be curious. Prepare answers to questions and comments you will likely hear, such as, "Take me with you!" or "I knew you weren't happy here," or "[boss] really is a jerk, weren't they?" Be respectful and don't speak ill of anyone on your way out. It may seem like it will be satisfying but it's not in your interest in the long run.

3. **Consider what projects you may need to wrap up and anything you want to ensure is finished before you go.** Work on these to ensure they end how you want them. Put files as appropriate on the shared drives if available, and clean up your email folders.

4. **Start preparing your staff for greater leadership roles** by having them step into meetings, learn about what you're doing, and ask questions so they learn. You can do this whether you've told them you're leaving or not.

5. **Prepare how you will tell people you're leaving.** I prepare a list of people I will tell in person (including my staff), people I will call on the phone, and people I will email. Remember, once you tell the first person, news will start getting out. I schedule all these meetings on the same day to have the leaving conversations, then make phone calls, and send the email at the end of the day. It will be an exhausting day, so make sure to plan something nice for yourself after work.

6. **If you've had a particularly awful work experience or if you struggle with transitions,** consider visiting a therapist or professional coach to work through challenges and help you let it go.

7. **Prep your friends/family outside of work to provide support to you during this time.** Ask for what you need.

8. **Consider little rituals that might help you close out the last chapter,** such as updating your resume or LinkedIn, getting new business cards or uniform at the new job, and celebrating with your friends.

9. **Remember there's a substantial emotional component to leaving a job.** Give yourself time to process changing your commute, losing some friends, leaving an employer you've known. Even if you're happy to move on, give yourself space for whatever feelings may arise.

10. **Reflect on your work experience.** What did you do well, what could you do better, what did you learn? Then let it go and step forward into the rest of your life.

See also: **Challenge 9: When and how to obtain a mentor**

                  Challenge 18: Build allies and friends at work

                  Challenge 24: Manage and overcome overwhelm

                  Challenge 25: Commit to continuous self-improvement

Take action: If you're ready to move on, start making a list now. Make lists of lists. Write down everything you need to consider, so you can get started.

Challenge 83.
Making sense of your career

Life is short, so take advantage of opportunities and live to the fullest. Life is also long, which gives us plenty of time to consider what patterns we have and what we have learned and contributed to others. It's a good idea to periodically review our careers to see how far we've come and identify where we'd like to go next.

1. **When you review your resume and see the jobs you've held, what patterns do you notice?** Have you had a direct line to the top? Wandered a bit? Tried new things? Whatever you've done, find pride in it.

2. **Consider each position and what you did at work.** What choices and achievements are you proud of? What choices do you not feel as good about? What can you do differently as you move forward?

3. **You may want to create separate resumes for different fields both for practical reasons and to see how far you've come in each area.** Check out resumes online to see what makes sense for you.

4. **If you were writing the story of your career,** what would it be so far? How would you like it to continue? What's next?

5. **Examine your network of professional and personal connections.** Did you generally stay in touch with people at previous workplaces? Why or why not?

6. **When you think back to 5 or 10 years ago, what did you want out of work and professional life?** Did you get there, or do you want something different now?

7. **How is your personal life?** Are there times when you didn't integrate work and the rest of your life as well as you'd like? How can you manage differently moving forward?

8. **What is your big dream?** How have you worked toward that? Some people have a dream of going to Paris, or being CEO, and don't realize how attainable the dream can be. It's a good time to address this big dream and start making it a reality.

9. **Ask senior leaders that you know to reflect on their professional life and the twists and turns their careers have taken.**

10. **Read about others' career paths.** Some good examples are books about Madeline Albright, Hillary Clinton, Bill Gates, Steve Jobs, and others who reached the pinnacle of their field.

See also: Challenge 9: When and how to obtain a mentor

Challenge 10: When and how to obtain a career coach

Challenge 24: Manage and overcome overwhelm

Challenge 25: Commit to continuous self-improvement

Challenge 80: Knowing when it's time to move on

Take action: Considering the above, write down what your next steps are toward the life you want. Add steps and a timeline—now you have a plan!

For further reading

These references include some of my favorites and some recent books that can help you along on your journey toward success and respect. Share your favorites at the Lead with Wisdom Community for Millennials on Facebook or send to me at Jennifer@leadwithwisdom.com.

Productivity

1. *Getting Things Done: The Art of Stress-Free Productivity* by David Allen. (Penguin Books, 2015).

2. *The Success Principles: How to Get from Where You Are to Where You Want to Be* by Jack Canfield (William Morrow, 2015).

3. *The 7 Habits of Highly Effective People: Powerful Lessons in Personal Change* by Steven R. Covey. (Free Press, 2004).

4. *How to Shine at Work* by Linda R. Dominguez. (McGraw-Hill, 2003).

5. *Tools of Titans: The Tactics, Routines, and Habits of Billionaires, Icons, and World-Class Performers* by Tim Ferriss (Houghton Mifflin Harcourt, 20160.

Self-Awareness, Self-Knowledge, and Understanding Privilege

1. *White Fragility: Why it's So Hard for White People to Talk About Racism* by Robin DiAngelo (Beacon Press, 2018).

2. *Own Best Friend: Eight Steps to a Life of Purpose, Passion, and Ease* by Kristina Hallett (Morgan James Publishing, 2019).

3. *Understanding White Privilege: Creating Pathways to Authentic Relationships Across Race* by Frances Kendall. (Routledge, 2012).

4. *You Are a Badass: How to Stop Doubting Your Greatness and Start Living an Awesome Life* by Jen Sincero (Running Press, 2013).

Communication and Negotiation

1. *Emotional Vampires: Dealing with People Who Drain You Dry* by Albert J. Bernstein. (McGraw-Hill, 2001).

2. *Influence without Authority* by Allan R. Cohen & David L. Bradford. (John Wiley & Sons, 1991).

3. *Influence: Science and Practice* by Robert B. Cialdini. (Pearson, 2003).

4. *Power Listening: Mastering the Most Critical Business Skill of All* by Bernard T. Ferrari (Portfolio, 2012).

5. *Getting to Yes: Negotiating Agreement without Giving In* by Robert Fisher & William Ury. (Penguin Books, 2011).

6. *The Five Dysfunctions of a Team: A Leadership Fable* by Patrick Lencioni (Jossey-Bass, 2002).

7. *Bargaining with the Devil: When to Negotiate, When to Fight* by Robert Mnookin. (Simon & Schuster, 2010).

8. *No More Team Drama: Ending the Gossip, Cliques, and Other Crap that Damage Workplace Teams* by Joe Mull. (CreateSpace Independent Publishing Platform, 2018).

9. *The Lost Art of Listening: How Learning to Listen Can Improve Relationships* by Michael P. Nichols (Guilford Press, 2009).

10. *Difficult Conversations: How to Discuss What Matters Most* by Douglas Stone, Bruce Patton & Sheila Heen. (Penguin, 2010).

11. *The Asshole Survival Guide: How to Deal with People Who Treat You Like Dirt* by Robert I. Sutton. (Houghton Mifflin Harcourt, 2017)

12. *Stop Complainers and Energy Drainers* by Linda Swindling. (John Wiley & Sons, 2013).

Personal Growth and Change

1. *What Color is Your Parachute? A Practical Manual for Job-Hunters and Career Changers* by Richard N. Bolles (Ten Speed Press, 2019).

2. *What Should I Do With My Life?* by Po Bronson (Random House, 2002).

3. *What Do You Want to Do When You Grow Up? Starting the Next Chapter of Your Life* by Dorothy Cantor. (Little, Brown and Company, 2001).

4. *The Power of Habit: Why We Do What We Do in Life and Business* by Charles Duhigg. (Random House, 2014).

5. *What Got You Here Won't Get You There* by Marshall Goldsmith. (Hyperion, 2007).

6. *Switch* by Chip and Dan Heath (Crown Business, 2010).

7. *What's Stopping You? Why Smart People Don't Always Reach Their Potential and How You Can* by Robert Kelsey. (Capstone Publishing Limited, 2011).

8. *Fear and other Uninvited Guests* by Harriet Lerner. (HarperCollins, 2004).

9. *Personal Development for Smart People: The Conscious Pursuit of Personal Growth* by Steve Pavlina. (Hay House, 2008).

10. *Tiny Beautiful Things: Advice on Love and Life from Dear Sugar* by Cheryl Strayed. (Vintage, 2012).

11. *Leading Exponential Change: Go beyond Agile and Scrum* by Erich R. Bühler (Innova 1st Publishing, 2018).*Women Who Dared by* Jeremy Scott (OneWorld Publications, 2019).

12. *Harvard Business Review's 10 Must Reads on Change Management* (Harvard Business Review Press, 2011).

Leadership and Politics

1. *Survival of the Savvy: High-Integrity Political Tactics for Career and Company Success* by Rick Brandon & Marty Seldman. (Free Press, 2004).

2. *Built to Last: Successful Habits of Visionary Companies* by Jim Collins & Jerry I. Porras. (HarperCollins Publishers, 2002).

3. *Good to Great: Why Some Companies Make the Leap . . . and Others Don't* by Jim Collins. (HarperCollins Publishers, 2001).

4. *Ask a Manager: How to Navigate Clueless Colleagues, Lunch-Stealing Bosses, and the Rest of Your Life at Work* by Alison Green. (Ballantine Books, 2018).

5. *Managing to Change the World: The Nonprofit Manager's Guide to Getting Results* by Alison Green & Jerry Hauser. (Jossey-Bass, 2012).

6. *Managing with Power: Politics and Influence in Organizations* by Jeffery Pfeffer. (Harvard Business School Press, 1992).

7. *The Secret Handshake: Mastering the Politics of the Business Inner Circle* by Kathleen Kelley Reardon. (Doubleday, 2000).

8. *It's All Politics: Winning in a World where Hard Work and Talent Aren't Enough* by Kathleen Kelley Reardon. (Doubleday, 2005).

Millennial Issues

1. *The Millennial Money Fix: What You Need to Know About Budgeting, Debt, and Finding Financial Freedom* by Douglas Boneparth & Heather Boneparth. (Career Press, 2017).

2. *Stuff Every Graduate Should Know: A Handbook for the Real World* (Stuff You Should Know) by Alyssa Favreau. (Quirk Books, 2016).

3. *Broke Millennial: Stop Scraping By and Get Your Financial Life Together* by Erin Lowry. (TarcherPerigree, 2017).

4. "Digital Natives, Digital Immigrants" by Marc Prensky. Available at Marcprensky.com.

5. *Millennial Money Makeover: Escape Debt, Save for Your Future, and Live the Rich Life Now* by Conor Richardson. (Career Press, 2019).

6. *Choose Your Own Adulthood: A Small Book about the Small Choices that Make the Biggest Difference* by Hal Runkel. (Greenleaf Book Group Press, 2017).

7. *I Will Teach You to Be Rich: No Guilt. No Excuses. No B.S. Just a 6-Week Program That Works* by Ramit Sethi. (Workman Publishing Company, 2019).

8. *Millennials' Guide to Work: What No One Ever Told You about How to Achieve Success and Respect* by Jennifer Wisdom (Winding Pathway Books, 2019).

Acknowledgments

I have such an amazing group of friends and colleagues who helped with this book, knowingly or unknowingly. Former bosses have been amazing laboratories in which to learn how to lead, struggle, try to be your best, sometimes fail, and generally succeed in helping your team and achieving goals. Some were amazing role models I still strive to emulate; others showed me the dark side of leadership when it is twisted to protect an ego or punish others. Thank you all for your lessons.

I especially want to thank the following superb leaders and managers who demonstrate integrity, power, knowledge, and kindness: Lynette Arias, Paul Atchley, RuthAnn Atchley, Michelle Berlin, Danielle Berner, Mira Brancu, Tracie Collins, Jennifer DeVoe, Lisa Dixon, Arthur Freedman, Carla A. Green, Lisa Guay-Woodford, Kristina Hallett, Sharon Heinle, Sarah Holland, Lisa D. Jenkins, Lynn Kunkel, Liberty Bird Martinez, Yvonne Michael, Shari Miles-Cohen, Doug Nixon, Alison Noice, Alma Starks, Liz Travis, and Shandra White.

Consultants improved the book immensely. Many, many thanks to Linda Warnasch, Valerie Weaver, Shandra White, Dick Kilburg, Georgette King (Hi, Mom!), Remember Watts, and the ever-impressive Cassandra Blake. Your thoughtful reviews helped strengthen the book substantially.

I wish to thank Brian Sisco at 115 Studios for cover design, Deana Riddle at Bookstarter for book design, Margaret McConnell for editing, Martha Bullen for marketing advice, Diego G. Diaz for photography, and Cassandra Blake for ideal administrative assistance.

Finally, amazing friends helped keep me going regardless of how I felt. They continually remind me of how many people need this kind of help as they become managers and leaders. Thank you: Katrina Amaro, Tara Amato, Lourdes Blanco, Chuck Chagnon, Diego Diaz, Jennifer Felner, Prea Gulati, Kristina Hallett, Sunny Istar Lee, Mary Mitchell, Billy Monks, Valerie Weaver, and Laura Zorich.

CPSIA information can be obtained
at www.ICGtesting.com
Printed in the USA
BVHW041935220920
589388BV00015B/806

9 781733 097734